Becoming Sacred

A Woman's Journey to Healing,
Transformation & Soft Power through
Sacred Feminine Energy

Lorrie Ann Fluker

Table of Contents

How to Use This Book

A woman's handbook for healing, transformation and soft power through sacred feminine energy.

"There comes a point in time when you realize that the thought of remaining the same may carry more pain and suffering than the unknown, so you evolved."
Lorrie Ann

Open Meditation: Please close your eyes. If you are not comfortable with closing your eyes, I invite you to just lower your eyes to a soft gaze. Slowly inhale and exhale. Inhale and exhale once more. Now, just notice your breath. While breathing naturally and silently, ask yourself these soul questions: Who am I? Why am I here? What do I want to gain from this experience?   Please feel free to journal your answers to these questions when you're finished with the meditation.

Now, slowly open your eyes and notice yourself returning to your body and surroundings, ready to receive...

Dedication

To my beloved and radiant daughter and granddaughters.
You are living testaments to the strength, grace, and
wisdom that flows through our bloodline. May your lives be
a celebration of the sacred feminine.

To my mother, whose journey, resilience and unwavering
love shaped the woman I am today.
To my grandmother, aunts and the matriarchal ancestors
whose names I may not know, but whose spirits walk with
me still, I carry your prayers, and transform your pain into
soft power. This work is an offering to your memory and a
continuation of your sacred path.

To the women standing at the edge of transformation.
May you feel the call of your divine essence and arise with
courage.
You are the midwives of a new earth, ushering in balance,
beauty, and wholeness.
We are healing, remembering, and becoming sacred
together.

Foreword

Lorrie Ann Fluker has raised her voice to help other women discover their sacred feminine power and divine design. Keeping silent no longer, she has emerged to speak her truth with clarity, conviction and guidance to existing and emerging generations.

Becoming Sacred is a book of depth, powerful wisdom and a clarion call to reconnect with your true identity, honor, value and self-worth.

Lorrie writes with a voice that is both ancient and timely, weaving personal truth, ancestral memory, and collective yearning into a sacred offering. As you turn each page, you may find yourself breathing more deeply, standing more firmly, and feeling more whole.

I have watched the emergence of this work in awe and witnessed Lorrie's transformative life journey. She took the time, did the interior work to gain insight, healing and freedom.

To the women on the path of remembering, to the healers, artists, and visionaries ready to shape a new earth: this book is your mirror and your guide. May it stir your soul and heal your identity.

Linda Wallace
CEO & Founder
A Company of Women

Linda Wallace's core belief is that women are an integral part of every thriving society. She has dedicated her life to helping women transform into their complete, unique, and powerful selves.

Introduction:
My Journey and Awakening to Sacred Feminine Energy

I was raised by a single mother who was born into a powerfully resilient matriarchy in the Deep South. The patriarchal structure of the state of Alabama has long since represented systemic oppression, particularly for black people, women and other marginalized communities. Patriarchy wrote and exacted the rule of law that gave shape and form to family and community structure within my mother's small town of Demopolis, Alabama.

Patriarchy, southern traditions and social hierarchies formed rigid governmental structures that reflected and favored toxic masculine behavior patterns while suppressing emotional expression in the Deep South.

Government, political and judicial leadership while wielding its hard power through the law had the audacity to make it illegal to react to the emotional and physical abuses that emasculated, exploited and oppressed black people as well as women.

This was a level of power that robbed many souls of autonomy, impacting them emotionally, physically, socially, politically and economically.

Although it allowed black women more access than their male counterparts in order to further divide and disempower the black family and community.

My mother once told me of being able to meet with the bank manager after hours to obtain a loan, because of the influence of her aunt who owned a popular cafe in town.

She wanted to buy a fancy new car, but she told the bank manager that it was a practical car, the same as his, in order to win his favor.

She was able to secure a loan using that tactic along with being a relative of one of the best known businesswomen in town.

My great aunt's cafe generated a lot of revenue serving blacks on one side and whites on the other in the small town of Demopolis. Folks would travel from neighboring counties to dine there.

Although black women and men lacked the freedom and autonomy necessary to live life on their own merit in general, many of them such as Madam C. J. Walker, the first female millionaire who was also black, used their intuition, creativity and other tools from their sacred feminine arsenal to achieve their goals.

Black women have always maneuvered in a way that capitalized on patriarchy's need to maintain control in order to evolve economically, maintain status quo and satisfy external ideas of success and power.

While doing so they sometimes abandoned their own emotional and physical needs, leaving behind a legacy of unnurtured and emotionally underdeveloped children.

We live inside systems that shape how we think, be, and carry ourselves. Some of these systems are divine, like the human body and the cosmos. Others are man-made constructs, conceived for control rather than connection, suppression and oppression rather than autonomy, creativity, interdependence and freedom.

Chief among them, patriarchy, a governing system, subtle and loud, ancient and ever-present. It is not just a political idea; it is an energy that has seeped into our bones, our wombs, and our voices.

The family dynamic crumbles under a toxic patriarchal system.

In every culture touched by patriarchy, there exists a hidden cost, one that ripples quietly through families, generations, and the souls of those within them. Patriarchy promises order, strength, and leadership. But in practice, it too often delivers rigidity, fear, oppression and emotional starvation.

At the heart of this dynamic is toxic masculinity, a distorted form of masculine energy that suppresses emotion, detests balance, enforces dominance, punishes vulnerability and leads with an iron fist and hard power.

Toxic masculinity tells parents to lead with control, not compassion. It teaches sons that sensitivity is weakness. It teaches daughters that their value lies in submission.

It is the root of emotional absenteeism and generational silence.

This toxic energy compels trauma and unspoken wounds to be swept under the rug and provides hurting souls zero knowledge of how to heal.

Over time, these beliefs fracture communication, stunt emotional intelligence, and create environments where intimacy and vulnerability are feared rather than nurtured.

My grandparents' union didn't survive the inherent emotional dysfunction. My grandfather left, leaving my grandmother with five young daughters ranging in age from adolescence to infant.

The family survived after being abandoned by their father with the hard work and sacrifice of my mother and aunts who merged forces in order to help my grandmother make "ends meet" and provide for their own necessities and desires.

My mother and her eldest sister supported each other's educational and professional pursuits as well as those of their younger siblings, while making many sacrifices along the way. They broke down barriers and blazed trails for the next generation to do the same.

My grandmother, mother and two of my aunts migrated north to Chicago in order to provide family support and further realize their professional aspirations, while the others headed west to realize entrepreneurial pursuits and expand the family's territory.

I am incredibly thankful for their hard work, sacrifice and dreams of a better life for themselves and their children. Inevitably, the perpetual grind of the masculine sphere can become an impediment to sacred feminine wisdom.

The nurturing, compassion and patience needed to cultivate healthy families and communities are often replaced by material things that are of no real consequence, and only serve to provide a momentary thrill and shot of dopamine.

You can not serve from an empty cup. Your health and that of your family will suffer. In her role of provider, my mom, like many women, was laser focused on education, career and financial resources while providing the material things that she perceived to be necessary in order to be well respected, embody good self-esteem and thrive in life.

However, those external masculine pursuits can leave women somewhat hardened, severely lacking in the areas of emotional balance and the sacred feminine energy that is critical for self-regulation and the spiritual enlightenment necessary to attain wholeness and wellness.

In an attempt to demonstrate love, self-worth, or success, parents in patriarchal societies and void of emotional intelligence in many cases offer gadgets, clothes, curated photos, or performance based praise instead of deep emotional presence, deep listening, and soul nourishing connection. Although it's not deliberate neglect, it's very often a reflection of their own unmet needs or unhealed wounds.

Children won't remember the brand of their shoes, they'll remember whether they felt safe, seen, and protected. When love becomes transactional, even unintentionally, it creates a void where sacred connection should be. It is this connection masked by outward abundance that contributes to emotional instability and spiritual hunger in the next generation.

Reclaiming sacred feminine energy in parenting means returning to the essence of nurturing the quiet, steady power of love that holds space for change, protects innocence, and nourishes the soul from the inside out.

Emotional and physical health and wellness, and sacred transformation have become my life's pursuit. My ability to recreate and transform after traumatic events is my superpower. My God power. My soft power!

Acknowledgment of emotions was taboo in my family as in society in general. Not overtly, but it's embedded in patriarchal code. Whatever energy impacting societal and cultural norms on the macro level will always be projected onto life on the micro level.

My need to be heard, validated and emotionally supported as a child was often compared to the harder and more traumatic experiences of our ancestors which seem to make my experiences and struggles pale in comparison.

During my formative years, emotional needs weren't worthy of attention, or validation. I learned to shake it off, suck it up and get over it rather than how to process emotions, heal from the ones that hurt and invite more of those emotions that healed me and brought great joy.

Those are skills that require conscious awareness, honesty, vulnerability, and the emotional intelligence that are considered as weaknesses in patriarchal societies.

My capacity and power as a woman had been impeded before I was even born by the deliberate suppression of sacred feminine energy throughout every systemically imbalanced patriarchal system of the world.

How could I have known that I would be born into a world of predetermined roles and boundaries, absent of the understanding of my true human and spiritual identity as a sacred energetic being? How could I have prepared for it once I'd arrived?

SACRED (Intentional, Devoted Force and Dedication)

Energy is sacred because it is the essence of creation, the force that animates all life, and the bridge between the seen and unseen realms. In its purest form, energy is divine; it is the breath of existence, the pulse of the universe, and the source from which everything emerges and returns.

The sacred feminine is deeply and inextricably linked to energy as creation. Whether through the cosmic womb, the cycles of nature, or the intuitive power within, sacred feminine energy is the force that births, nurtures, and transforms. It moves in spirals, in waves, in unseen currents, shaping reality with fluidity and grace.

Sacred feminine energy cultivates emotional intelligence, creating a space where feelings are acknowledged and validated rather than diminished. This helps families and communities feel secure, making it safe for open and honest communication and emotional resilience.

When women lead with nurturing, patience, intuition and creativity which is the foundation of sacred feminine energy, it creates an atmospheric frequency that can facilitate healing, and forgiveness, and encourage autonomy and self-expression.

Sacred feminine energy is also deeply connected to ancestry and the wisdom of past generations. Honoring family lineage, healing inherited trauma, dis-ease and embracing traditional wisdom strengthens familial bonds and roots the family in a sense of purpose and direction.

Many families prefer to just sweep family trauma caused by emotional, physical and psychological abuse "under the rug." They do so, because they simply don't possess the emotional intelligence, information, or tools to heal the wound, or mitigate the threat of continued trauma.

Feminine energy is not a trend, a social aesthetic or a device to manipulate romantic relationships, it is an ancient, divinely sacred force that has existed since the beginning of time. It is the energy of creation, intuition, nurturing, and transformation.

Reducing this powerful energy to just a way to attract a partner or to live a life of opulence and entitlement diminishes its true power and purpose to not only transform yourself on a micro level, but to also transform the world on a macro level going far beyond the realm of ego and ascending to conscious awareness. Christ consciousness.

I am a daughter, mother, and grandmother. I have loved and experienced great loss. I am a teacher, philosopher, metaphysician and deep thinker. I know that I've come to this experience called life to be a vessel of change and to share transformational wisdom through enlightening information that might support the inner evolution of women. Transformation isn't possible without creativity, acceptance and detachment. None of the aforementioned could be possible without feminine consciousness and energy.

Throughout history, there have been periods and cultures where women were worshiped for their ability to bring forth life and held significant power. The creative capacity of women has enabled humankind to survive, and also to thrive. Ancient societies revered female deities, centering their religions and cultures around their divinity. The sacred feminine was synonymous with fertility, creation, and the nurturing aspects of life. Archaeological evidence, such as Venus figurines, suggests that prehistoric societies honored women as embodiments of life force energy. These figurines symbolized fertility, motherhood, and the abundance of the earth. In these early civilizations, a woman's ability to give birth and sustain life was seen as not only powerful but magical. A force of nature.

This reverence for the sacred feminine has been buried under centuries of suppression, yet our power has never left us. It has been covered up like so many sacred places on the earth, but our lost rituals, wisdom, and soft power lives in our bloodlines, in our bodies and in our quiet spaces of remembering.

The feminine arsenal is fully equipped to transform both inner and outer worlds with the tools she holds deep within herself. She holds within her deep listening, intuitive knowing, creative force, emotional intelligence, sensual wisdom, and regenerative power. Sacred feminine are sacred technologies. While the world has long celebrated force and domination, it is the feminine that teaches us how to recalibrate, restore, and to lead with guided wisdom.

In the hands of an awakened woman, compassion becomes strategy, nurturing becomes activism, stillness becomes revolution and creativity promotes inspired action that is necessary to set humankind on an evolutionary journey of rebuilding through love, creativity, intuition and acceptance.

A woman's perceived weakness is the greatest illustration
of society's misunderstanding of her power. The feminine
is not lacking. She is emerging and she is ready to conspire
with the universe to create a new earth.

I've discovered that my true power isn't forceful—it is
intuitive, fluid, and deeply connected to divine wisdom.
Ease and grace, acceptance and detachment gently and
gracefully aligns me with my ground state of conscious
awareness. It is within this conscious state of awareness
that I find peace, joy, rest and resolve. Anytime I dare to
venture too far from this ground state, I descend into
survival mode, imbalance, and ego. The ego state is easy to
return to, because I've practiced it all my life. The ego is
rooted in illusion, separation, and survival-based thinking.
It is necessary for navigating the material world, but when
it dominates, it disconnects us from our true, divine
essence.

Many of my ancestors were never given an opportunity to
ascend beyond the ego state that exists in the evolutionary,
survival codes within the human DNA. They were in a
constant state of fight or flight.

That state supports basic survival, but isn't coded to
support inner evolution, or the ability to holistically thrive.

It has taken me many years, and many experiences to learn
that by raising my consciousness, surrendering to the
source of my being, and embracing my sacred feminine
energy, I can access goddess energy and soft power. I have
become a witness to my own actions and desires, giving
them my full attention. I now understand that I have no
need to lend energy to things I do not desire, nor do I need
to judge or resist them. I use what I do not desire as
contrast to move me toward my desires and
manifestations.

Where attention goes, energy flows like a current. A
current is a circulating force, a flow of intention, energy,

and value. Just like energy, currency is neutral until directed. It can build, heal, destroy, or transform based on how it's used.

Energy changes matter and creates the material world. You use money (currency) to buy things that give shape and form to your life and your environment on a physical level such as a new home, food, clothing, etc.

On a metaphysical level: Your personal energy (your inner currency) influences your reality. Joy, confidence, fear, gratitude, creating a flow that shapes outcomes.

I am practicing mindfulness around using this currency wisely.

Why I Wrote This Book

I have been following and practicing various aspects of holistic healing for over twenty years. My introduction to holistic based wellness and healing began over thirty years ago. My son was born with end stage renal disease due to a structural defect. He began receiving peritoneal dialysis treatments at only six months old and received a kidney transplant at fourteen months. My goal was to learn everything I could to support his overall health and wellbeing. I found a great holistic/ homeopathic doctor who taught me about integrative medicine, healing and how supporting the body's natural balance would allow it to heal itself. That experience led me to Deepak Chopra and Ayurveda. I started becoming more enlightened through reading his and others books and listening to teachers of eastern philosophies on various audio and visual platforms. I applied all that I'd learn to the health of my son and family. My faith grew strong and when my son left this world I was promised, "beauty for ashes." I am bound to that promise every day that I live.

I began to notice a common thread and a consistent systemic theme standing in opposition to wellness. Emotional imbalance and lack of conscious awareness are the stressors that erode relationships, health and wellbeing through family generations. Balance is the creator's divine strategy to not only sustain life, but make it more abundant.

Throughout my adult life I've experienced insurmountable hurt, fear, and disappointment, while trying to invite joy, contentment, encouragement, and optimism. I strived to make what was difficult appear seamless in the eyes of my children.

I was carrying the entire emotional and spiritual weight of this difficult experience alone. My loved ones and friends supported my family as best they could, but when the doors closed and the lights were turned off, I would drown in my own tears on the pillow. Each day I had to find renewed strength and resilience, a new reason to smile.

I decided to become the woman I believe myself to be. I focused on surrendering all to the universe. I discovered that the only true power I had was that of allowing things to be what they are in every moment and in every season.

I learned that when I focused on the external, I felt powerless, but when I set my intention on what I could do internally to create joy, acceptance and consistency it alleviated stress and things began to flow and work together producing more desirable outcomes.

Stress is the common thread at the root of most diseases, but lifestyle is at the root of stress. The material world is in opposition to our ground state and patriarchy governs how we navigate the material world from a flawed premise. Toxic masculinity rules from a place of fear, lack and greed. This energy chases resources instead of acknowledging wholeness. Wellness and natural rhythms are replaced by a constant state of survival, fight or flight. Cortisol is a stress hormone magnificently created to support human survival, but causes significant dysfunction in all systems of the body when it is unable to stabilize.

Living in a chaotic and constant state of strife, and unrest while chasing external pleasure and material gain stands in opposition to the development of true identity as a co-creator and a loving, compassionate steward of the earth.

I was thrilled when I learned that there was an opportunity to train in Ayurveda, a healing system dating back over five thousand years under the brilliant, spiritual and wise guidance of Deepak Chopra and his phenomenal team of teachers and practitioners. This experience has truly been what I was seeking. It has carried me back in time to the root of my existence and state of being. Remember, what you're seeking is always seeking you.

The Law of Attraction is the scientific explanation of this spiritual event. The Law of Attraction is the principle that like attracts like, and the energy you put out into the world shapes what you receive in return. It's based on the understanding that thoughts, emotions, and beliefs act as energetic signals, influencing your reality.

Energetic alignment is how a divine marriage of mind, body and spirit is possible. Two becoming one goes far deeper than the physical. In sacred wisdom and philosophy, an energetic marriage is not about possession or control but about divine co-creation with the balance of feminine and masculine energies.

Sacred feminine energy is the soft magnetic force that brings what you desire to you. It's divine law!

I am Soft Power, is a sacred feminine community and platform that connects women who want to transform their lives by becoming more aware of their inner purpose and power and learn sacred practices that integrate emotional, spiritual and physical wellbeing through Ayurveda and the marriage of sacred feminine and masculine energy.

I believe that by experiencing this journey of enlightenment, you will learn how to embrace and cultivate a sacred balance within that will attract the relationships, experiences and opportunities that are your energetic match, allowing you to create your own reality and the boundless life you desire. This level of autonomy and self-love will not only transform you, but it contains the power to transform the material, 3D world as you know it.

Ayurveda is a healing and wellness system that has supported optimal health, wellness and emotional balance for over 5000 years. Ayurveda helps me become more intentional and aware of emotional and physical imbalances as they occur, while intentionally and continually inviting wellness and balance into my being through Ayurvedic practices that align mind, body and spirit. Women are often in a state of imbalance due to various life demands. The truth is that human beings are always feeling our way back to our ground state through our own internal emotional guidance system. Sacred feminine energy is a powerful recalibration tool in maintaining a healthy, life sustaining temperature and homeostasis.

I believe that women are the hearth of the home and have long been regarded as such. A sacred woman is a constant burning fire that is necessary to provide warmth, comfort, nurturing and healing to her family and community, because of the divine spark of life giving and nurturing, sacred feminine energy that she both transmits and emits.

Life depends on the home fires continual burn not just in a physical sense, but in a deeply energetic and spiritual way. Just as a fireplace is the hearth of the home and the kitchen is the heart of a home, a woman's sacred feminine energy represents the life force embers that keep the home fires burning providing nourishment, nurturing, physical and spiritual growth, comfort and transformation.

Becoming Sacred is the first of what I hope to be many written offerings from my platform.

I am a certified Ayurvedic health and wellness teacher with the Chopra Institute of Integrated Health and the Institute of Integrative Nutrition. I am a student of my practice, and I implement Ayurvedic wellness rituals in many forms everyday. Letting go of old patterns isn't easy. There are societal programs that dictate to us what to eat, drink, think and believe all day everyday. These programs and patterns affect individuals, families and communities, generationally. Wellness practices help me to transmute unwanted energies into ones that serve me and help me maintain my ground state in the midst of life's challenges with ease and grace which are both frequencies rooted firmly in sacred feminine energy. Join me on my journey of transformation and support the reemergence of sacred feminine power.

The world is in crisis, and women are an intricate part of the solution. For too long, the thirst for power, perception of lack and mindset of greed have distorted our understanding of existence and poisoned our minds, leading many to believe that fear, lack and discord are naturally occurring elements of life. Yet, everything in nature whispers a different truth. One of abundance, balance, renewal, and limitless possibility. Mother Earth does not struggle to bear fruit, the rivers do not force their flow. Abundance and peace are not external pursuits to be obtained, they are a conscious state of inner awareness that assists in returning us to our ground state.

We cannot survive on bread alone. The material world is not our source; it is merely the outward expression of our collective inner thoughts, beliefs, and actions. To truly thrive, human life must be nurtured in the body, mind, and spirit. Yet, modern society has conditioned us to believe that power must be forceful, that strength is found in dominance, and that success is earned through struggle and being alone is the same as loneliness. I have learned a different truth: my power is not in force, but I possess soft, transformative, healing power that flows with the natural rhythms of life and is accessed while alone in quiet meditation and noticing nothing but the sound of my breath and during deep creative states.

The feminine arsenal is powerful—not in ways the world has traditionally recognized since the rise of patriarchal societies, where femininity was often relegated to domestic roles, but in ways that transcend force. We have the ability to disarm with patience and understanding, to influence through love, to protect without aggression, to nurture without depletion, and to build through creativity and collaboration. A woman's perceived weakness is, in reality, a profound misunderstanding of her nature. Softness is not fragility. Surrender is not submission. To embrace the sacred feminine is to align with the life force energy that animates all of creation.

I have discovered that my truest power is not in resistance but in allowing inspired action. When I operate from a state of non-resistance and acceptance, I am not only at peace—I become a vessel for abundance, healing, and transformation. This is my natural state, my ground frequency, and from this place, I can manifest the world that I desire, effortlessly.

I wrote this book to help women return to sacred feminine and re-member their true identity, divine power, and purpose that has always been their birthright. Through sacred knowledge, ancient wisdom, and wellness practices that integrate the mind, body and spirit. I invite every woman to reconnect with the soft power that has the potential to connect you to your highest self, shift your mindset, cancel generational contracts and create a new reality. A new heaven and earth begins with you. You possess the power to bring heaven to earth.

It is time to awaken. It is time to return. It is time to align.

PART I:
Recognize The Wound

Chapter 1:

The Impact of Patriarchy & Hard Power on Identity and Wellness

As far back as I can remember, I have questioned everything. I remember asking my mother when I was four years old, "Are we special?" I can still remember asking the question and the answer that followed over fifty years later. The question that poured out of my innocent and untarnished soul, void of conditions, found its answer in the response from a woman whose soul had been riddled by many of life's conditions—racism, classism, sexism, and every other ism, schism, and divisive energy cultivated in the patriarchal, Jim Crow South. All of her diminishing programming unconsciously rose to the surface that day.

My soul was excited and desperately yearned to hear words of affirmation and confirmation that would match my inner knowing, my feeling of uniqueness, privilege, regality, and abundance. My mother looked at me and responded out of her experience and societal programming: "No honey, we're no better than anyone else." She didn't want me to be hurt like she had been by haters who had judged her shine as uppity and arrogant.

Her ancestors had been brutally reminded that freedom was something they'd receive when they died and went to "heaven", love came with conditions, potential was framed by the lies of those who owned them and exploited it and they had no "self" to esteem.

Her response came from a good place, a protective place that had been subliminally downloaded into her mind through religious dogma and societal norms—a belief that unwittingly disconnects one from their own unique identity, autonomy, and sacredness.

A Legacy of Survival and Sacrifice

I was raised by a single mother born of a strong matriarch from the Deep South—Alabama, a training ground for white male supremacy and entitlement. The patriarchy wrote and exacted rule of law. In the Deep South Jim Crow esq., was the name of the ignorant, divisive, and mean spirit of this toxically, imbalanced masculine energy that dominated the law, politics, religion and society at large. It demeaned and oppressed and had no understanding of true abundance, or the beauty of humanity and inclusion, or creation.

Although it can be said that my hardworking and ambitious matriarchal ancestors had overcome some of the restraints that the grip of Jim Crow had over their lives, it wouldn't be an honest assessment to describe it as thriving. They were surviving under suppression that was normalized in their everyday lives. There was certainly an emotional and psychological toll to be paid while enduring such systemic oppression of being both black and a woman in southern society.

My family eventually did what many oppressed and marginalized people in the world do, they set out to find better opportunities in a land where they might realize their dreams. The formidable matriarch made the journey from Alabama to the big city of Chicago during the second Great Migration of Black folk who were descendants of enslaved people in America. This was a larger migration than that of the first migration. It involved over five million descendants of enslaved Africans in America. It extended beyond the North into the West to cities like Los Angeles, Oakland, and Seattle.

They arrived in Chicago armed with education, hopes, dreams, and a pretty intense work ethic generated by their desire to remain in authority over their lives amidst unrelenting adversity.

The feminine arsenal was present in every step of that journey, nurturing families, overcoming systemic violence with focus and attention to detail, and transforming the fabric of American life through grace, inspired action and generational wisdom. This migration was a sacred movement, both literally and spiritually.

They were in various stages of life and womanhood. Many years prior, my mother and her sisters had been abandoned by their father, and the eldest of the five girls were obligated to garner their collective grit and co-parent with their mother. They worked, sacrificed, and helped their mother provide during the season of their lives when they needed to be nurtured and supported. They endured hardship while working in their aunt's café and in the homes of well-to-do white folks while finishing high school and college. They supported each other's endeavors and managed to maintain a good reputation in their small community. They continued being a supportive family in Chicago.

They bought a small home on the South Side of Chicago. My mother was eight months pregnant with me and had already secured a teaching job in Alabama. My eldest aunt,

with her two children and husband, was seeking
employment in her field of study. My grandmother
intended to see my mother through her pregnancy and my
birth, because she had recently separated from my father.
My aunt also needed my grandmother to support her
family in Chicago. My grandmother wouldn't leave for
Chicago without my mother agreeing to the move. My
mother sacrificed her career to support her sister and move
to Chicago just as her sister had worked and sacrificed to
support her earlier in her educational pursuits.

There were many sacrifices made in the coming years that
affected both my mother and myself. I learned that
self-sacrifice was something that was expected, but I also
witnessed the resentment and regret it can sometimes
create.

Self-sacrifice, when rooted in obligation rather than
overflow, can quietly breed resentment. While the world
often praises the "strong Black woman" archetype for how
much she can carry. She has been branded a "mule".
Self-sacrifice rarely pauses to ask what she needs. True
sacred feminine energy does not demand depletion—it
invites balance, reciprocity, and reverence. The sacred
feminine gives, but not from an empty cup. She knows that
martyrdom is not ministry. When we abandon our own
nourishment for the sake of others, we step out of
alignment with our divine design. Sacred power is soft and
it flows from fullness, not fatigue. Choosing yourself is not
selfish—it is a spiritual act.

Barriers To Feminine Balance

The cost of being a "strong woman" is high, and the price is often paid through the loss of feminine energy and consciousness and over compensation of masculine energy. Emotional balance and surrender, nurturing and patience, creativity and receptiveness of feminine energy was sacrificed for independence and logic over feeling, hustle and control, and emotional detachment of masculine energy. As was the case of my matriarchal line. The necessity of "doing" and suppressing emotions was needed for survival, but the tranquility found in just "being" and honoring emotions was a luxury that the women of my matriarch simply could not afford

It was my curiosity and questioning of these generational, cultural, and societal norms that would allow me to explore how I viewed womanhood. Questioning those norms opened up a portal within me. It gave me permission to explore how I had internalized womanhood not as a birthright, but as a burden. I began to untangle the scripts and programming I had inherited: that to be a woman was to serve without rest, to love without boundaries, and to endure without truly being seen or heard. In this unraveling, I uncovered a sacred truth. Womanhood in its divine form, is not about conforming, it's about becoming. It is fluid, intuitive, cyclical, powerful and invites wholeness.

By questioning what I was taught and by watching what was happening all around me, I began to remember my authentic truth and identity.

The Rise of Patriarchal Energy

There was a time when the Earth was honored as Divine Mother. When intuition guided the village and the moon marked our rhythms. The womb was seen as the seat of creation and not a burden, but a blessing.

But something shifted. Not all at once, but slowly, forcefully, and deliberately.

The sacred feminine was not erased. She was buried. Like so many artifacts, ancient libraries and evidence that connect humankind with their true origin, identity and divinity.

Systems of Sacred Feminine Suppression

Patriarchy is not just a system. It's an energy, a wound on humankind and a distortion of balance. It is a governing system sending messages that has shaped how we see ourselves, how we value our bodies, and how we access power. Everything within and outside of ourselves has a governing system.

Patriarchy works like the nervous system, sending messages through every institution, every family line, every standard of living.

The messages come early, encoded in our education, media, and even spiritual traditions. They train the body to shrink, to serve, to be still unless spoken to. They numb us to our own sacred knowing.

Under patriarchy, identity becomes performance.

Wellness becomes productivity and femininity becomes something to be fixed, hidden, or controlled.

Bloodlines and Privilege: The Circulatory Flow of Power

In a healthy body, the circulatory system nourishes every part equally. No organ is left starving, no cell forgotten. But patriarchy clogs the flow. It sends power and privilege to a select few, while others are forced to survive on scraps.

It's not just about gender. It intersects with race and class, creating a caste of neglect and invisibility of some and overexposure of abundance and presence of others.

I will never forget my grandfather's funeral. I had learned much about him from my grandmother. I learned that he was a smart man, but conflicted. As far as I know he was raised by women who were very protective of him. My grandmother had shared with me that her family had warned her against marrying him. My grandparents had a tumultuous relationship. It was largely because of misalignment of their core beliefs. Personal identity, societal roles and toxic masculinity created space for emotional and physical abuse and neglect. He didn't want my grandmother to work. They had five children and my grandfather being a Black man in the Deep South in the 1930s and 40s was relocated to domestic work. He worked as a house manager (house boy) for a white family that owned insurance companies and sold cars.

While my grandfather was managing another man's family for a living, his own went without his presence and emotional support. My grandmother would later work for an insurance company and become a licensed practical nurse in order to support her family alone. My mom and her sisters worked in their aunt's cafe as I mentioned before. They worked hard and were even taken advantage of by those who were supposed to be helping them. Their aunt and uncle often withheld their pay saying they hadn't made enough to pay them. One of my aunts knew that the strong box that had collected the day's earnings was hidden in the floor and helped herself to the money and paid all of them what they were due.

When my grandmother would receive word that my grandfather was coming home she called everyone home. My grandfather had forbidden any of them to work. When he returned home everyone was there, leaving him with his toxic form of pride along with the control he couldn't access anywhere else.

Eventually he stopped returning home, withdrew his money from the bank and later had his aunt retrieve the refrigerator.

My mother and her sisters were still in elementary and high school at the time. When word got out about this travesty the town folk began talking. When one of my aunts arrived at school one morning, her teacher announced what had happened in front of the class. They later discovered that their father had another family. Needless to say, there was a root of low self-esteem planted that day and a block in energetic flow.

Abandonment, whether physical, emotional, or spiritual, creates profound disruptions in a child's energetic flow. From the earliest stages of life, a child's energy system is in a state of rapid development, closely tied to feelings of safety, belonging, and connection. When a primary caregiver withdraws, disappears, or becomes emotionally unavailable, it interrupts this flow, leading to blockages, imbalances, and long-term wounds that can affect the child's body, mind, and spirit.

Trauma causes invisible blocks in places that cause breath to shorten, posture to tighten, voice to quiet or become loud and disruptive, and self-worth erodes. Over time, these energetic interruptions begin to shape how we see ourselves. We start to confuse survival patterns with personality and normalize pain as identity.

However, this isn't the truth of who we are. We are beings that have access to sacred feminine energy and the sacred feminine knows how to flow, express, release, and rise. When we begin to heal, we aren't just restoring our energetic balance, we are restoring our self-esteem, our sovereignty, and our sacred connection to our inner divinity that is God.

At the energetic level, children are open fields, highly receptive, deeply sensitive, and vibrationally attuned to their environments. Healthy energetic flow depends on consistent love, affirmation, and presence. These create a stable foundation for the root chakra, which governs feelings of safety, trust, and groundedness. When abandonment occurs, that foundational energy center is shaken, often leading to an internalized belief that the world is unsafe, unreliable, and that love is conditional or fleeting.

This disruption does not merely affect emotional development; it fractures the flow of life force energy throughout the body. The heart chakra, for instance, may constrict to protect the child from future hurt, leading to difficulties in forming intimate relationships later in life. The solar plexus chakra, tied to personal power and self-worth, may weaken, resulting in struggles with self-esteem, agency, and confidence.

I met my father once. My mother and father separated before I was born. I overheard conversations about who he was, but discussing him with me was forbidden. However, comparisons to him were made of me by my mother on occasions when my behavior was deemed as selfish as a little girl. Before meeting him, I would imagine who he might be. A famous singer, a professional athlete, a politician maybe. Even after meeting him, I didn't know him. My uncle knew him and always wanted me to connect with him, but the idea was never backed up by any actions that would assist me in doing so. He lived in Alabama and I later discovered that he had sired many children in that small town.

I believe that having an opportunity to know my father and make my own assessment of who he was or was not to be in my life may have proved purposeful. Clarity and understanding brings us back to center, to balance. When the mind is unsure and emotions are tangled, there's a feeling of unsteadiness, and overwhelm. As a result, many of my decisions in life may have been different, and formed from a stronger emotional base rather than a broken one.

Children who experience abandonment often unconsciously adapt their energy to survive. Some may energetically "collapse," withdrawing inward to minimize the pain of rejection.

Others may develop hypervigilance, energetically reaching outward in search of approval and connection, depleting themselves in the process.

Both responses are attempts to stabilize disrupted energetic circuits, but they come at the cost of authenticity, ease, and true self-expression.

The nervous system doesn't lie. When safety is absent whether through violence, neglect, or emotional suppression it reacts. In homes shaped by toxic masculinity, where dominance replaces dialogue and emotional needs are dismissed as weakness, family members unconsciously adopt survival responses: fight, flight, or freeze. These are not flaws. They are strategies for survival in an environment where tenderness and compassion are absent and vulnerability is unsafe.

All of these disruptions can pass down generationally if not addressed.

My mother had an opportunity to reconnect with her father later in life. They went on trips together and enjoyed a renewed relationship. When my grandfather advanced in age and was no longer able to manage his affairs alone he turned to my mother. She supported him until the end of his life. It wasn't easy and in fact, the stress of it negatively impacted her health.

When I arrived at my grandfather's funeral in Mobile, Alabama and entered the grand mortuary where my mom and I were looking for the parlor where he lay waiting to be memorialized, I was shocked to see a parlor filled with white folks.

I sat down feeling like an outsider. I listened for over an hour as one generation after another of the family he'd worked for talked about how much fun they had with my grandfather and how nurturing and caring he had been. They told stories of his good cooking and how much they trusted him. The elder of the family shared how he would fly ahead of him to open up their summer home making it lovely for them to enjoy. He even helped drive the cars across the country to their dealership.

I was furious, because his own children got what was left over and my mother seemed content at that moment.

My grandfather's sacred masculinity was cut off from his own family, but flourished within the family where he was compelled to perform at his highest level. Leaving them feeling loved and cherished.

To become sacred, we must restore the flow, making sure our voices, our visions, and our healing reaches every part of our being, and every corner of our community.

Systems of Sacred Feminine Suppression

Have you ever noticed how patriarchy defends itself? Like an immune system misfiring, it attacks anything unfamiliar: feminine leadership, softness, emotion, freedom. It labels them as dangerous, irrational, or weak, but what patriarchy rejects is often what heals us. Tears cleanse. Surrender strengthens. Pleasure reclaims. These are not threats— they are medicine.

As Above, So Below: Cosmic Systems and Sacred Order

The universe has its own rhythm. Planets orbit not by force, but by harmony. Stars burn because of inner ignition, not domination. The cosmos honors balance, relationship, autonomy and interdependence.

Patriarchy seeks to dominate, extract, conquer. It resists flow. It fears softness. It forgets that everything sacred is cyclical.

We are not here to orbit around power. We are here to embrace power, soft power, the kind that restores, expands, and creates worlds.

The Identity Wound

Patriarchy teaches us to define ourselves by external validation.

- To be good, not whole.
- To be pretty, not powerful.
- To be quiet, not wise.
- To be useful, not sacred.

This disconnects us from our intuition, our cycles, and our body's language and rhythm. We begin to see softness as weakness. Rest as laziness. Emotion as instability.

I can remember Saturday mornings growing up in the 70s. After completing a full week of school and work, Saturday mornings presented me and my mother with more work which is normal practice in our culture. It wasn't a time for rest and recalibration. It was another day of work, housework. Although I had chores to complete everyday, Saturday was a deep cleaning day. My mom and I worked on the lawn, washed the car and cleaned the entire house. Our home was perpetually clean and shining. I wasn't allowed to sit on beds once they'd been made, or lean on walls. My Saturday tasks were to be completed by noon. I couldn't leave the house before my chores were completed.

My mother, like many women, although not always conscious of it, was very concerned about measuring up. I totally understand how this evolution occurred. As a Black woman in America she didn't have the luxury of being mediocre while still having access to opportunities. She knew that she was judged on a much higher level than her white female counterparts. In her mind, everything had to be "just so". Perfectionism ruled and there wasn't much space for rest.

I was bound to comply, but you can believe that noon found me dressed for the day and heading outside where my real life awaited. I looked forward to being able to visit friends, enjoy laughter, sit on made beds, lean on walls and enjoy being free to make my own decisions. Everyone desires autonomy even though we weren't all, born free.

Sundays met me with another day of experiencing my life through a pre-planned event not of my choosing, but that of subconscious patriarchal conditioning and control. I grew up in the Baptist religion where there was emphasis on rules, sin, guilt and obedience, typically to male authority. The tone and tenor of the preacher's voice resonated fear and judgment.

My religious experience in childhood was intimidating, yet very entertaining in retrospect. I enjoyed the theatrics of the choir director as she conducted the music of a creative and musically gifted Black choir. We had the thrilling antics of folks catching the Holy Ghost and the gossip of who was the pastor's side piece in that season. The deacons and administrators kids were spilling the tea.

There was a lovely teenage girl who led the youth and young adult choir. I'll never forget how excited I was when she chose me to share what she was prepared to do to get the attention of a really handsome usher of whom she was smitten.

I was probably eleven years old. She said, "I'm going to catch the Holy Ghost so he can come and see about me." WOW! She began to shout exclaiming, "Thank you Jesus." I couldn't believe it when she shouted, danced and jumped partially out of her shirt revealing her pretty lace under garment. Sure enough he came over, hands gloved carrying a fan in hand. He whisked her away. She didn't return until church was nearly over.

Her mom was a single mother of three daughters who, like myself, experienced the rituals and expectations of patriarchy's idea of a good girl. Some girls were resolved enough to secretly live an autonomous lifestyle while simultaneously going along with the life they hadn't chosen for themselves. The quiet rebellion worked for some, but sent others straight into the arms of those hunting women who were wounded and seeking attention.

Many women have been programmed to seek external affirmation, but true power is in the self-esteem that is found in self-awareness and grounded in conscious awareness.

Never forgetting that we are sovereign. Never forgetting that we are sacred.

The Wellness Distortion

In a patriarchal lens, wellness becomes another hustle, another thing to strive toward.

- Green juices, but no space to breathe.
- Gym bodies, but no space for grief.
- Healing that looks good, but never touches the soul.

Women's insecurities are profitable. The beauty, diet, fashion, and even some aspects of the wellness industries profit from making women feel they must "fix" themselves.

In today's world, "wellness" has been stripped from its roots and rebranded into something performative, commercial, and often violent to the sacred feminine body.

True wellness is spiritual wellness and is not about control.

I realize that my mother, although a hard worker and definitely leading with her masculine energy out of necessity, also cultivated certain aspects of feminine energy that were conveyed to me by omission. She believed in looking beautiful and attractive, being healthy, maintaining a spiritual practice and expressing herself creatively. She still does at ninety-five. She had and still has subscriptions to all of the beauty and fashion magazines. I had a subscription to essence and seventeen magazines. They were my holy grail of self-care and beauty.

Although she invested great time and effort to consciously manifest her physical beauty, ironically she would downplay her efforts by refuting compliments and seemed to be uncomfortable with the attention she attracted.

We inadvertently send the universe mixed messages creating misalignment and confusion about what we wish to attract when we fail to ground ourselves in conscious awareness and become a silent witness to our own being.

I can remember finishing my chores on Saturday to finally submerge into a hot bath with my magazines. I did my nails, skincare routine, etc. before going out to light up the world, giving and receiving beautiful energy in the way a young goddess should. Through enjoyment, pleasure and delight.

If I had known then, what I know now, I would have remained devoted to myself. I would have understood that self-devotion is a perfect point of attraction. The universe is a mirror that reflects the love you have for yourself back to you in endless, beautiful forms. The energy called God resides within you. When you love yourself, you love God. Expressing love is the greatest service on earth.

It's about divine alignment and connection.

It's about embracing your body as a temple, not as a machine or device for someone else's pleasure or purpose, but as an altar of devotion to your highest self and your creator, and a place where you conjure your own reality from strong desire.

Understanding Energy as the Source of Life

Every living being, from the tiniest cell to the vast galaxies, is powered by energy. This life force—called prana, chi, or kundalini in different traditions—is sacred because it sustains existence itself. Without energy, nothing moves, nothing grows, and nothing transforms.

Energy is not bound by time or space; it flows endlessly, shifting from one form to another. This eternal, unbreakable cycle reflects the sacred nature of energy—it is the unchanging force behind all change.

The patriarchy is more than just a social structure—it is an energetic system that has shaped the way we interact with power, creation, and the sacred feminine. It is built on hierarchical, controlling, and dominance-based energy, which disrupts the natural flow of balance, intuition, and divine connection and perverts the mind.

How Patriarchy Disrupts Our Flow

The patriarchy doesn't just govern politics or pay gaps, it lives in our everyday beliefs. It's in the glorification of burnout. The pressure to hustle. The fear of rest. The belief that receiving is selfish, but this isn't your truth, it's conditioning.

We often overthink rather than trust our gut. We silence our inner "no" to agree with someone else's 'yes". We even ignore signs, dreams, or intuitive nudges that are guiding us toward truth. It disconnects us from our sacred feminine energy, the part of us that nurtures, trusts, feels, flows, and receives.

And because money is also energy, when we suppress the feminine, through control, fear, shame, or disconnection, our ability to receive is blocked and we disrupt our natural relationship with abundance. We begin to believe that earning must be hard, that we must struggle to deserve and our worth is tied to how much we produce.

I have heard stories and experienced firsthand what happens as a result of not trusting my intuition, that gut feeling. My mother once told me about a series of dreams she had prior to marrying my father warning her to call it off.

I've often ignored the subtle inner voices that served as warnings to me to turn around, or that encouraged me to move forward in pursuits that might positively affect my life.

Spending time in meditation and prayer is a practice of learning to become familiar with the vibration and voice of your higher self, the voice of your god self. The more time I spend in silence, the more I trust that inner knowing.

Dissolving the Old, Birthing the New

In physics, entropy is the natural unraveling of closed systems. When energy becomes too rigid, too over-controlled, it begins to break down. This is where patriarchy finds itself now fraying at the edges.

And this is why we awaken.

We must seek balance in all things in order to not only survive, but to thrive.

The left and right hemispheres of the brain are often associated with different cognitive functions, and many spiritual and psychological traditions link them to masculine and feminine energies.

Masculine energy helps you see your goal and focus on it and hit your target. It's what I call "the hustle." It enables you to apply physical effort in order to achieve your goal. When out of balance, it attempts to force the natural flow of life. It often leads to burnout, stress, and mental breakdown. Unlike the masculine, which seeks control, the feminine embraces trust, cycles, and divine timing. Sacred feminine energy takes inspired action. Feminine energy embodies creative energy because it is the life force power of creation. I call it "the juice", the sweet nectar of life.

The sacred feminine operates beyond logic, trusting gut instincts, dreams, deep knowing and "aha" moments. It is the force behind life itself, not just in childbirth but also in the manifestation of ideas, art, and transformation. Feminine energy is the source of creation. It manifests and creates life and new worlds through sensuality and sexual alchemy. It is so powerful that in the beginning, man worshipped it and protected it. Our power and protection are in our divine feminine energy, the true nectar of the gods.

Transformation Through Sacred Feminine Wisdom

Sacred Affirmation: "I am ready to reclaim my feminine power and step into my highest self. I'm thankful for divine cooperation."

Sacred Feminine Practice: Sit quietly for five minutes and listen deeply to yourself. What is your intuition telling you?

Sacred Reflection: What does 'Sacred Feminine' mean to me? How have I experienced it or its suppression in my life?

Sacred Prayer:

Divine Mother, She who weaves stars and soil into sacred rhythm,

Breathe into me your holy wisdom.

Teach me to flow, to feel, to fiercely love.

May I remember the priestess within me,

The healer, the warrior, the nurturer.

Let my voice be truth,

My body be your temple,

My life be a ceremony.

I surrender the illusion of separation.

I return to the sacred.

I return to myself.

And so it is.

Chapter 2:

The Power of Feminine Energy

(Feminine Energy: Divine, Creative, and Restorative)

Understanding the Sacred Feminine

Women are capable of wielding great power through the device of attraction and influence. Your true power lies quietly and unassumingly, within where sacred codes of the divine feminine unlock soft power. It can not be found while looking outside of yourself where ego rules. The feminine arsenal is fully equipped to disarm. It is nurturing, accepting, and intuitive, and uses emotions as a guidance system. I've often heard the wise elderly women in my community comment: *"If men are the head then women are the neck that turns the head."* This statement is a vivid explanation of the disarming influence held within the sacred feminine realm.

Conscious awareness and wholeness is your ground state and it is the key that unlocks the sacred feminine realm. It is a space where intuition, receptivity, creativity, and nurturing are honored as divine intelligence.

The Sacred Feminine is a divine, creative, and life-giving force present in all human beings, regardless of gender. It represents the cyclical aspects of existence, flowing in harmony with nature, emotions, and spirit. This energy is the counterpart to the Sacred Masculine, and together, they create balance and wholeness in both individuals and the universe.

The feminine embraces the full spectrum of emotions, seeing them as a source of power rather than weakness. It fosters deep relationships with others, nature, and the divine through love and compassion, detachment to outcomes. Understanding the origin and usage of masculine and feminine energy is a powerful key to life. Balancing the two is necessary in order to self regulate, cultivate healthy relationships and take the inspired actions that will profoundly impact your inner evolution and the evolution of humankind.

The concept of evolution without inner spiritual growth leading to devolution suggests that while humanity might advance technologically and materially, the lack of corresponding spiritual and ethical development can result in a regression in terms of societal well-being, moral integrity, and overall human fulfillment.

Our patriarchal society seems to pride itself on the creation of tools of mass destruction and other mechanical and architectural trophies that show proof of its success, but give little consideration to how the creation and disposal and decomposition of all these material tokens affect the environment and the wellness of the people that depend on it.

All of creation, from human beings to plant life, can exist without the many material trappings of so-called success, but it cannot exist without clean nontoxic water, healthy fertile soil and clean unpolluted air.

There is no transformation without the surrender, creativity, and compassion of feminine energy and consciousness. Feminine energy is divine. Understanding the purpose and power of feminine energy will change everything you have ever been taught about womanhood. Society has given us broken bits and pieces of information about femininity. Feminine energy allows space for reconsideration, reconciliation, and restoration. It is creative, accepting, and intuitive. It is the power before the action. It takes inspired action that is nurturing and considers the protection of creation rather than the exploitation of it. It understands the abundance of the earth and supports and protects her.

Sacred feminine doesn't stand in opposition with man-made weapons to fight patriarchy. It is much obliged to outgrow it, outlove it, and outlast it through the vast and unlimited sacred feminine arsenal.

We do this by healing our bodies, reclaiming our wisdom, and remembering that we are systems, too — divine ones. Connected to the Earth. Aligned with the stars. Alive with purpose.

Sacred Affirmation: "I am not governed by fear. I am governed by sacred law. I flow like the universe. I rise like the sun and I am becoming sacred."

The Dance of Energies: Harmony Between Feminine and Masculine

Masculine energy without the inspiration and consideration of feminine energy is dangerous. It is born of ego, perceives everything and everyone as a threat, it's toxic and is only concerned with survival. Feminine energy without masculine energy can never give birth to what's been conceived. The purpose and power of the human experience is in the balance and harmony of the two.

Authoritarian fathers that have full control without compassion are examples of masculine leadership without feminine inspiration. In a family setting, many fathers that I've encountered have maintained strict discipline, believing that control and authority were paramount in parenting. His children and wife however, felt emotionally neglected and feared open and honest communication. Over time, this led to strained relationships and apathetic behavior. For years, his wife implored him to actively listen, show compassion and nurture his family, but without the energetic marriage of masculine and feminine emotional balance and resilience isn't possible.

Young men face societal pressures to conform to hyper masculine ideals like stoicism, dominance, and suppression of emotions. This has led to tremendous internal conflicts, depression, and difficulty forming authentic relationships. There are too few examples of men that model emotional intelligence, spiritual depth, and relational leadership. Instead, patriarchal controlled media often glorifies hyper masculine figures focused on power, conquest, and self interest.

The Sacred Dance of Masculine and Feminine is the divine union where polarity becomes harmony. It is the original rhythm of creation—sun and moon, structure and flow, doing and being. Neither energy is superior; they are meant to complement, awaken, and elevate one another.

The Sacred Feminine is the womb of intuition, emotion, creation, sensuality, and flow.

The Sacred Masculine is the spine of presence, protection, direction, clarity, and grounding.

Together, they create a sacred rhythm. Masculine holds space while feminine fills it with beauty.

Feminine opens portals of feeling while masculine gives those feelings direction.

When the dance is balanced in relationships, there is mutual respect. The feminine feels safe to express and expand, and the masculine feels honored in his role to hold, guide, and protect.

Within our inner being, we become whole, acting with both intention and intuition, soft power and compassion, logic and emotion. We lead and we listen. We initiate and receive.

Each time I've prepared to purchase a new home, I've set a plan in motion. I started happily saving money toward that end. By applying inspired action the savings seemed to accumulate faster than normal and extra resources showed up unexpectedly. I would also start watching design shows, movies that reflect my creative ideas and researching apps that provided creative visuals for how my house was to become my home. Masculine energy obtained the house, but feminine energy made it my home in a most desirable way.

If faith is the substance of things hoped for and the evidence of things unseen, then desire is the root of faith. Desire provides a reason to believe, have faith and never doubt. It creates the vision. Inspired action is the labor that gives birth to the vision.

Feminine dreams while masculine builds. Feminine feels while masculine listens. Feminine flows while masculine anchors.

The most beautiful relationship that I could imagine is one where each person is seen, heard, honored and appreciated. That relationship allows for mutual contribution and co-creation. Masculine appreciates the dreams of feminine and feminine honors the work and sacrifice of masculine. Both male and female embracing the masculine and feminine they each possess.

Within the collective community we heal. We move from domination to cooperation, from hierarchy to harmony. Society thrives when both energies are equally valued.

When this sacred dance experiences trauma, the wounded masculine becomes controlling, rigid, emotionally cut off and the wounded feminine becomes overly dependent, chaotic, or self-sacrificing. The dance turns into a battle. One energy tries to dominate or suppress the other, rather than move in rhythm together.

While you're experiencing this in relationships, it's difficult to recognize exactly what is happening. You find yourself frustrated, exhausted and hopeless. Making it through the day with uncertainty about when the next explosion of toxic emotions might erupt becomes a normal state of being. Everyone's physical and emotional health is at stake.

Restoring the Sacred Dance through rituals that honor both energies in daily life will help invite inner healing and wellness to everyone. Practicing stillness and movement, giving and receiving, work and rest will create harmony.

Practice listening deeply, holding presence, and allowing your partner (or yourself) to flow in both masculine and feminine essence without judgment.

Through inner union reclaim the parts of you that were silenced. Allow your feminine to feel fully. Allow your masculine to lead with heart and inspiration.

The Sacred Energetic Dance is not static, it's a spiral. It evolves with you. It doesn't ask for perfection, only your presence.

When we allow both energies to arise, we become whole. We remember we are not meant to fight our polarity, but to move with it like breath and heartbeat. Feminine and masculine energies, while spiritual in essence, also have correlating expressions in the brain's structure and function.

Feminine Energy in the Brain is often associated with the right hemisphere, which governs: Creativity & Intuition.

The right brain is nonlinear, imaginative, and connected to imagery, mirroring the feminine's deep intuitive wisdom and emotional sensitivity.

Empathy & Emotional Processing

The limbic system (especially the amygdala and insula) is more active in emotional attunement, often stronger in women, and tied to the sacred feminine's ability to feel, nurture, and connect.

Relational Awareness

Feminine energy thrives in relationships and interconnection. The mirror neuron system and feedback helps us empathize and emotionally sync with others, key to the feminine's gift of holding space and sensing needs.

Holistic Thinking

Right-brain dominance also supports seeing the whole picture, rather than linear steps. It is an intuitive pattern of recognition that reflects the feminine's cyclical nature and spiritual depth.

Masculine Energy in the Brain is often associated with the left hemisphere, which governs logic & linear thinking.

The left brain focuses on analysis, structure, and step-by-step problem-solving—echoing the masculine energy's focus on direction, order, and purpose.

Goal Orientation & Action

The prefrontal cortex plays a major role in planning, discipline, and decision-making—tied to the masculine's role as the initiator and protector.

Risk Assessment & Control

Structures like the dorsolateral prefrontal cortex are involved in impulse control and strategic thinking, reflecting the masculine's boundary-setting and leadership qualities.

Task Separation & Focus

Masculine energy excels in singular focus and compartmentalization—an asset in leadership, defense, and progress.

Both energies live in all of us.

Healthy brain function means being able to access both hemispheres fluidly, integrating intuition and intellect, logic and love, structure and surrender.

Women have greater access to both. The corpus callosum, which connects both hemispheres, is key. Studies show it's often more developed in women, supporting fluid communication between masculine and feminine energies. But anyone can strengthen this balance with mindfulness, creative practices, emotional attunement, and embodied rituals.

Women carry influence when guided by the Sacred Feminine energy. A Sacred Feminine realizes that her power is soft. Soft power isn't weak but understands that matter doesn't change matter. Energy changes matter, and energy was never created, nor can it be destroyed, it simply takes different forms. Those forms are shaped by thought, creativity, and inspiration from a ground state of abundance and wholeness, rather than fear and lack. The processes of manifestation and/or transformation are from within.

In a world often divided between doing and being, structure and flow, force and nurture, there are women who show us what it means to embody both the sacred feminine and the awakened masculine. Among them, Dr. Wangari Maathai stands as a luminous example.

Born in Kenya in 1940, Wangari grew up deeply connected to the land. The forests, rivers, and soil were not just resources to her, they were relatives. This reverence for nature was the feminine within her: intuitive, relational, and rooted in care. But as industrialization and deforestation swept across Kenya, Wangari saw her beloved landscapes turn barren. Streams dried. Women walked miles to find firewood. The Earth and its people were losing their balance.

And so, she acted.

But she didn't respond with rage or aggression. She moved with fierce compassion. In 1977, she founded the Green Belt Movement, a grassroots initiative led mostly by women, planting trees and restoring the land. The feminine spirit guided her vision—healing, nurturing, creating community. But it was her masculine energy—her courage, structure, and discipline—that carried it forward.

She lobbied government officials. She challenged corruption. She faced imprisonment. She was beaten and publicly ridiculed. Still, she stood tall—not as a woman hardened by power, but as a woman embodied in balance. She used her voice as a sword and her heart as a shield. Her masculine defended her feminine; her feminine gave soul to her masculine.

This integration was radical. It defied gender expectations. It also healed thousands of acres of land and empowered rural women to become stewards of their own futures.

Wangari Maathai's life teaches us that balance is not about choosing one side of ourselves—it is about becoming whole. The sacred feminine invites us to care, feel, and dream. The sacred masculine gives those dreams form, structure, and protection. She showed us that leadership doesn't have to imitate dominance—it can be rooted in love.

By the time of her passing in 2011, over 50 million trees had been planted because one woman listened to the Earth and dared to respond—not just with heart, but with hands. With both intuition and action. With the fullness of her being.

In her, the dance of balance was restored. And in her story, we are reminded that we too, can lead, softly and powerfully. We are led to believe that we are powerless to make and sustain systemic change in the world. People even mimic the words, "You can't change the world." Everyone seems to be looking for a leader to come and save them. You are that leader!

An Imminent Threat: Why Do Systems of Power Fear Sacred Feminine Energy?

In a world shaped by conquest, colonization, and control, the sacred energies that dwell within us all—feminine and masculine—have long been distorted, repressed, or weaponized. These sacred forces are not about gender, but about divine principles that, when balanced, bring harmony to individuals, communities, and the planet.

Toxic masculinity creates significant imbalances in a woman's life physically, emotionally, mentally, and spiritually.

Patriarchy, with its toxic masculine energy runs programs to divide and interrupt sacred feminine consciousness, shifting focus away from the feminine strategies such as reasoning, recognizing the power of emotions to attain understanding, utilizing inspiration, collective collaboration, and creativity to find solutions to common problems.

Governing systems without balance disrupt the balance of nature and the planet. Patriarchy, and its toxic masculine idealisms overtly and covertly programs women to be competitive, preferring "the hustle" and accumulation of things, over compassion and service to the wellbeing of humanity.

The Sacred Feminine is the greatest threat to hard power. Feminine power decentralizes control: It honors the collective and the cyclical, which threatens rigid, top-down power structures. A feminine model says power with, not power over—and that's revolutionary.

Sacred Feminine consciousness leans toward appreciation and abundance. When these energies are suppressed, people suffer. Relationships become power struggles. Communities become battlegrounds. Institutions become cold and extractive. And the inner world becomes a war zone, as individuals lose access to the fullness of who they are and their ground state.

The fear held by patriarchy for Sacred Feminine is not about the feminine being inherently "weak" or "threatening" in an aggressive sense. Instead, it stems from the recognition that the Sacred Feminine represents a complete reimagining of power—one that is decentralized, holistic, collaborative, and grounded in the rhythms of nature and the spirit. This is why society is programmed to view women as weak while systematically stripping them of power.

The patriarchy suppresses feminine energy because it disrupts control-based systems. Sacred Feminine is often viewed as a threat to the patriarchy, but not in a combative sense. Rather, the Sacred Feminine challenges the core principles that underpin patriarchal systems, such as domination, control, linearity, and hierarchy. When women and individuals begin to embrace and embody the sacred feminine, it disrupts the patriarchal narrative and restores balance in ways that can feel threatening to those in power who benefit from maintaining the status quo.

Feminine energy embodies intuition, creativity, emotional depth, and sacred connection. It challenges hierarchy with collaboration and holistic wisdom.

Matriarchal governance embodies the wisdom of the Sacred Feminine, using soft power to build relationships, resolve conflicts, and create sustainable communities. In today's world, embracing these principles can redefine leadership—shifting from control and hierarchy to cooperation, intuition, and nurturing strength.

The healing lies not in flipping the power dynamic, but in restoring harmony. The feminine must rise, but not to replace the masculine. She must rise to meet him. And the Sacred Masculine must awaken not to conquer, but to co-create with the feminine.

This is a spiritual revolution. It begins within.

The Iroquois Confederacy: Women as the Keepers of the Nation

Long before European colonization, the Iroquois Confederacy (Haudenosaunee) of North America developed a sophisticated political system that inspired parts of the U.S. Constitution. Central to this system were the Clan Mothers—respected elder women who appointed and removed male chiefs and ensured that governance aligned with the needs of the people and the earth. Their leadership upheld principles of peace, environmental stewardship, and intergenerational responsibility. The matrilineal structure ensured that power remained grounded in family and community rather than concentrated in individuals. "Individual fingers can be broken, but a fist can knock out an opponent."

My matriarchal line was most powerful when the women worked as a team supporting and nurturing the entire family. They stood strong together against everything. The oppression that society would offer, supporting each other financially, but their emotional and physical health suffered, because sacrifice and labor can sometimes leave little space for self-love, or real self-care. Their own cup was rarely full and it's difficult to serve from an empty cup. They didn't share their emotional challenges. Those were held stoically within. Emotional suppression had been normalized for generations.

Sacred Feminine was suppressed leaving only the energy of striving. I remember my mother sitting me down often to explain to me that life is hard. She said that she was "scuffling" to make "ends meet." Everyday held the energy of the fear of lack that had been coded in her DNA. I later experienced that same fear in my own family.

I was reminded in my own home along with my children that lack was our ground state and we shouldn't expect much beyond a roof, utilities and food. I now understand

62

that belief to have been programmed by the lies and fears of generations of lack.

I have always communicated my pain. In the same therapeutic way others used stoicism to cover theirs, I used communication to exorcise mine. I needed someone to tell me that they understood my trauma, but I've learned that my trauma belongs to me and my source, and no one is coming to save me. The only savior I'll ever know resides deep within me. Sacred practices provides balance and connection to my salvation, a state of conscious awareness where pure, positive, potential grounds me in truth leaving no space for doubt.

My mother always believed in balancing her affairs. She managed her money, time, relationships and leveraged each of them to have the quality of life that she desired for the two of us. She was an amazing provider, but it would be up to me to entertain myself and cultivate my own emotional wellbeing, because there wasn't much time, or intention placed there. I didn't realize how much of an impact that had on me until much later in life. I would have to transform my life at a really "big" age, while proving to myself that it is never too late to invite soft, transformational power into my life.

The Sacred Feminine threatens power-hungry systems because it invites change, flow, and transformation. External programs like religion, media, education and politics were shaped and formed to keep women disconnected from their inner light, abundance and power, but through sacred practices you are sure to return to the truth. Your capacity to create your life is within. As within, so without. As above, so below. You manifest from thought, intention, and inspired action.

Let Your Light Shine

We marvel at creatives and even call them stars. But they are simply aligned souls surrendered to divine feminine energy. They let their light shine. They use it to attract.

Matthew 5:15-16 (KJV): "Neither do men light a candle, and put it under a bushel... Let your light so shine before men, that they may see your good works, and glorify your Father which is in heaven."

Letting your light shine is Sacred Feminine. It means rising in your gifts, honoring your truth, and living from inspiration.

I am a powerful dreamer and manifesting those dreams are my delight. It just makes me happy and filled with joy to know that the universe and I are in divine partnership. I come from a line of magical women who dreamed and saw visions. When I was a young child, I would dream in sequels. Night after night I would fly across my city of Chicago. I perfected both my take off and landing. I can still remember how the top of my feet gently brushed across the treetops as I descended preparing to land. On my journey I met great people, stopped crimes and reformed criminals, attended garden parties and received lessons in humanity.

I loved the Jackson 5! I would dream of them practicing in my living room and performing for my mom and I.

I felt like they were a part of my family and although I had a crush on them, I was more interested in their impact on the world and how I could experience that level of influence and power.

As fate would have it, the universe conspired with me and I did meet them. Myself, my cousin and my childhood friends established the Jackson Jewels with their blessing. The Jackson Jewels was a community awareness organization helping young inner city girls to grow and evolve beyond the confines of their community and dare to dream of a bright future. It was very successful and was a stepping stone to great careers for many of the young ladies.

Sacred Feminine energy empowers dreams, overcomes oppression and makes space for the creation of abundant life.

Rewriting Her-Story: Reclaiming Feminine Identity and Influence

Historically, women have been stripped of their rights. They were denied voting rights, the ability to own property, access to education, professional opportunities, reproductive autonomy, and representation in leadership. Women were seen as property, confined to domestic roles, and used for male benefit.

Layla: Sold Online in the Middle East, 2016

Layla, a Yazidi teenager, was captured by ISIS and sold in an online auction. Her image, veiled and crying, was uploaded alongside dozens of other women and girls. She was traded four times, each man more brutal than the last. Her captors told her she was a spoil of war, a "gift from God" for their fight. Her cries were met with laughter. After months of captivity, she escaped with the help of a smuggler. She now lives in Germany and speaks publicly about her experience. "They thought they owned me," she says, "But I took back my story."

The oppression of women is the suppression of the Sacred Feminine. Demonizing emotions is how patriarchy maintains power. Healthy emotions are balanced and reasonable. The power of the patriarchy is dominance over reason, logic over intuition. This is the ultimate imbalance and pathway to the destruction of a human soul. Make a monster, get a monster.

Ephesians 6:12 reminds us: "Our struggle is not against flesh and blood, but… against the powers of this dark world and against the spiritual forces of evil in the heavenly realms."

Sacred Feminine Energy is a gift—a necessary catalyst for evolution. Women carry this in abundance. You bring healing and hope into the world. You are the hand and heart of God. If you understand source energy as God, the creator of all things, then you may understand Sacred Feminine Energy as Goddess, the co-creator.

The Systemic Impact of Patriarchy and Toxic Masculinity on Society

Toxic masculinity infused patriarchal societies affect all of creation. Male-dominated leadership often leads to exclusion, inequality, conflict, and imbalance. Male leadership has often created systems that ignore women's health, fail to address reproductive justice, and perpetuate hostile environments through toxic masculinity.

In patriarchal societies, feminine energy is often exploited rather than honored, leading to chaos, disruption of flow and suppression of its true power. Women around the world disproportionately carry the emotional, physical, and mental labor of caregiving—whether it's raising children, tending to aging parents, or supporting partners. This invisible labor can deeply affect their time, finances, careers, and well-being.

Women are often expected to provide emotional support, caregiving, and spiritual guidance without recognition, compensation, or reciprocity. Many women feel overburdened and taken for granted, but refuse to give voice to those feelings for fear of being labeled a complainer. Patriarchal societies make no space for emotional recognition.

Patriarchal systems prioritize logic, aggression, and competition over intuition, empathy, and collaboration key aspects of feminine energy often resulting in voices in leadership being dismissed as "too emotional" or "irrational."

In the 2024 U.S. presidential election, patriarchal programming—ingrained societal norms that prioritize traditional male dominance and masculinity—significantly influenced voter behavior and campaign strategies. The election highlighted pronounced gender divisions among voters. Data indicated that a majority of white women continued to support Donald Trump, with 53% backing him, mirroring trends from previous elections. This suggests a persistent alignment with candidates who embody traditional patriarchal values.

The 2024 election served as a microcosm of the broader societal struggle between entrenched patriarchal norms and the push for gender equality. The persistence of patriarchal programming influenced voter behavior, campaign tactics, media narratives, and policy discussions, highlighting the ongoing challenges faced by women and marginalized groups in achieving equitable representation and treatment in the political arena.

Media coverage during the election often perpetuated gender stereotypes. Female candidates like Harris received less coverage focused on policy and more on personal attributes, such as appearance and demeanor. This disparity reinforces traditional gender norms and diminishes the perceived legitimacy of women in politics. (The Australian) (Center for American Women In Politics)

Statistics show that gender equality in leadership reduces violence, increases diplomacy, improves emotional well-being, and fosters inclusive policy. Patriarchal systems devalue the Sacred Feminine by prioritizing power, productivity, and control.

Feminine energy is the source of creation. It manifests through sensuality, wisdom, and spiritual alchemy. Originally, man worshipped this power—but now, in many ways, women are exploited for it.

There was a sixties sitcom that I watched as a child called, *I Dream of Genie*. Genie was a pretty blonde genie that lived in a bottle that her astronaut boyfriend found when he crash landed in the Middle East. He would let Genie out of the bottle when he needed her, but ordered her back in her bottle when she overstepped her bounds.

You are not a genie in a bottle or a lamp, but that is a powerful image. Women as genies in a lamp or a bottle. Mystical, powerful, full of divine gifts... yet confined, summoned only to serve, and then shut away again. It captures how women's intuitive wisdom, emotional intelligence, nurturing power, and creative force have been historically exploited by patriarchal systems—used when convenient, but rarely honored or given space to flourish freely.

Her gifts become tools for someone else's agenda. Her light is bottled, her boundaries erased. The lamp becomes a symbol of both reverence and restriction.

In the early 19th century, a young African woman named Sarah Baartman was taken from her homeland under the illusion of opportunity and thrust into a European world that did not see her humanity—only her body. Born in South Africa in 1789, Sarah was later exhibited across Europe as the so-called "Hottentot Venus," paraded before crowds who ogled her curves, ridiculed her features, and dissected her very existence.

Sarah was exploited not just for her physical form, but for the deep feminine power she symbolized.

The curves of her hips, the depth in her eyes, and the softness of her presence were twisted into spectacle. Instead of revering her fertility, sensuality, and spiritual magnetism as sacred—colonial society commodified it. They exoticized her body, using it as a symbol of "otherness," stripping it of spirit, soul, and story. Her femininity was feared and fetishized. Her power was too great to be honored, so it was mocked and contained.

What they didn't realize was that what they tried to exploit was holy.

Sarah's story is not just historical—it's ancestral. It reflects how society has long attempted to control the divine feminine: by objectifying, sexualizing, and shaming it. For many Black women especially, Sarah's legacy lives on in the ongoing struggle to reclaim the body—not as an object of gaze, but as a vessel of wisdom, creativity, and sacred power.

While her body was exploited in life and even after death, what's rarely discussed is this: the shape of Sarah Baartman's body didn't just shock the Western world, it silently reshaped it.

The Corset and the Crinoline: Shaping the "Ideal" from Spectacle

In the decades following Sarah's exhibition, European fashion underwent a dramatic transformation. Women's clothing began to emphasize narrow waists, wide hips, and full backsides, an exaggerated silhouette that bore a striking resemblance to the very features for which Sarah was put on display.

Corsets became tighter, constricting the waist and lifting the bust to unnatural proportions.

Crinolines and bustles and undergarments made of horsehair, wire, or steel cages, were added underneath dresses to artificially extend the hips and backside, creating a shape that mimicked Sarah's natural figure.

What's deeply ironic and painful is this: Sarah Baartman was dehumanized for her curves, while white women were celebrated for artificially creating them.

The Sacred Reclamation

Though Sarah Baartman died in 1815, her remains were not returned to South Africa until 2002. The journey of her bones mirrored the journey of her spirit: one of remembrance, mourning, and reclamation. Today, she stands as both a warning and a call to action to protect the feminine, to remember the cost of disconnection, and to reframe our gaze from exploitation to reverence.

No, you are not a genie in a lamp! You embody the divine energy of creation and it's time to accept and embrace your role.

Transformation Through Sacred Feminine Wisdom

Sacred Affirmation: "I reclaim every part of me that patriarchy tried to silence."

Sacred Meditation:

- Close your eyes and bring awareness to your breath.
- Visualize a lotus flower blooming at the base of your spine.
- With each inhale, imagine its petals opening—radiating light, strength, and softness.
- Feel the energy rising through your womb, heart, and crown.
- Whisper or think: "I bloom in truth. I bloom in power. I bloom in softness."

Sacred Prayer:

Great Mother, Womb of creation,

Guide me back to myself.

Help me move through the world with tenderness and fire.

Let me walk in beauty, speak with truth, and rest in my softness.

I offer my wounds for healing and my wisdom for sharing.

I am yours, and I am whole.

Ase. Amen. So it is.

PART II:

Remembering the Truth & Returning to Power

Chapter 3:

Understanding the Imbalance

Living in the Shadow of Imbalance

The negative impact of imbalanced masculinity in male leadership in society is multifaceted, affecting interpersonal and family relationships, community, political representation, economic equality, workplace culture, health policies, and international relations and overall peace on earth. While male leaders are not inherently detrimental, the systemic issues associated with traditional masculine dominated energy in leadership structures often perpetuate inequality and conflict. Embracing Sacred Feminine Energy in leadership is crucial for developing more balanced, inclusive, equitable, and peaceful societies.

Societal roles set by the narcissistic behavior patterns of toxic masculine leadership are formed from a perverted understanding of the roles and responsibilities of a king.

The Distorted Masculine: From King to Tyrant

A true king, in the traditional and spiritual sense, embodies leadership rooted in wisdom, justice, and service. His role is not about domination but about protection, provision, and purpose—serving as a guardian of the land and its people. A king safeguards his kingdom, not through oppression but by ensuring safety, justice, and well-being for all, because he is compelled by stewardship and protection. He seeks wisdom and justice, leading with discernment, making fair decisions that uphold balance and honor truth. A king serves his people, understanding that leadership is a duty, not an entitlement. In many traditions, a king is deeply connected to divine will, embodying sacred wisdom and spirituality to guide his people.

A true king uplifts the Sacred Feminine, recognizing and honoring the divinity of the queen as his equal in power and wisdom, creating harmony in leadership.

Patriarchy has distorted the noble role of a king by replacing service with control, wisdom with domination, and balance with oppression. Instead of a protector and nurturer of life, the patriarchal king becomes toxic and tyrannical—using power to dominate rather than uplift, ruling with fear instead of wisdom. Toxic masculinity suppresses the Sacred Feminine. Instead of honoring the queen as a co-sovereign, patriarchy reduces women to possessions, stripping them of voice and influence.

The toxic masculinity and hard power in governance is rooted in caste and class systems. In these systems, people are ranked in order of importance based on bloodline and stature in society. Women have historically been on the bottom rung in patriarchally governed societies.

Symptoms of Cultural, Mental and Physical Imbalance and Internalized Oppression

Women often experience mental health issues such as anxiety, depression, frustration, and stress due to emotional repression in male partners, fathers, or colleagues, leading to a lack of emotional support, feeling unseen, and invalidated.

Women, especially in emotionally imbalanced or patriarchal dynamics, often become the containers for emotional weight that male partners refuse or are unable to process. When men repress their own emotional truths, women are often left to feel for two, constantly absorbing the tension, silence, and emotional labor of the relationship.

Lack of communication can be linked to the subliminal impact of hard power. Over time, this unreciprocated emotional burden can lead to nervous system dysregulation in women—chronic anxiety, burnout, depression, even breakdowns. The feminine, being deeply attuned to relational energy, often internalizes the disconnection and begins to unravel under the weight of what is unspoken.

Destabilization is the most favored tool of patriarchy! It works by creating confusion, doubt, and dependency especially in those who hold power within themselves, like intuitive women who are spiritually attuned.

Patriarchy gaslights intuition, labeling it "irrational" or "too emotional." Women often second-guess themselves, to seek external validation instead of trusting inner knowledge. Those who embraced their full Sacred Feminine power were often punished.

One clear historical example is the persecution of women during the witch hunts of Europe and Colonial America. Women who were midwives, herbalists, seers, healers, and those with a strong spiritual attunement were labeled as witches and brutally silenced. These women were often community pillars, helping others reconnect with nature and spirit through non-hierarchical, intuitive means. The targeting of these women was not random; it was a calculated move to dismantle alternative sources of wisdom and power that operated outside male-dominated religious and political institutions.

Religious institutions played a major role in destabilizing feminine energy. As patriarchal interpretations of spirituality became the norm, feminine archetypes were either demonized or sanitized. For example, figures like Mary Magdalene, once a symbol of spiritual strength and devotion, were recast as sinners to diminish the image of an empowered, spiritually astute woman. Goddesses and priestesses, once revered in ancient civilizations, were either erased or incorporated into male-dominated pantheons with diminished significance. These efforts systematically stripped Sacred Feminine wisdom from collective consciousness, leaving a void filled by rigid dogma that emphasized hierarchy, obedience, and masculine domination.

Eve is blamed for the fall of humanity casting women as the origin of sin. Eve is blamed in the Genesis story because her choice to eat the fruit from the Tree of Knowledge is framed as the moment humanity "fell from grace." But that framing is patriarchal interpretation—not divine truth.

This narrative destabilizes feminine wisdom, desire, and autonomy, branding curiosity and knowledge as dangerous when expressed by women.

Eve became the symbol of disobedience and temptation, setting a foundation for blaming women for sin, chaos, and disorder.

The fruit came from the Tree of Knowledge, wisdom, awareness, discernment.

Patriarchy painted the pursuit of knowledge (especially by a woman) as dangerous. They created the same religious basis to enslave and oppress my ancestors, making seeking knowledge punishable by death. Knowledge is the biggest threat to patriarchal control.

By blaming Eve, the story justifies male dominance. Adam is portrayed as a passive victim, and God's punishment puts Eve "under" Adam. Please understand that women were not included in writing these religious texts the same way my ancestors were not included as men when they wrote the patriarchal constitution.

Eve wasn't weak; she was curious, courageous, and awakened. She chose knowledge over blind obedience, which is the beginning of consciousness. My ancestors understood knowledge as freedom.

Eve's act could be seen as a sacred initiation into duality so that we could learn, grow, evolve. Contrast is necessary for utilizing free will. If we were given the gift of free will by God, why is the supposedly "god-fearing" white male patriarchal leadership so afraid of it? I believe that it's because it thrives off of the resource of energy that exists in every human being.

Your autonomy allows you to use that energy to thrive, thus becoming the authority and power over your own life. Patriarchy was created from the fear of lack. Because of the disconnect from feminine energy, spirit and ground state there isn't an understanding of freedom and abundance on their behalf.

Exploitation and control is the ego level of human beings, and supports our most basic need, survival. There is a contractual stronghold on the entire earth through colonization achieved with the Bible in one hand and oppression, loss of identity and autonomy in the other.

The "fall" was not a curse but a descent into an awakening and a necessary step in the soul's evolution.

Eve is blamed in the Genesis story because her choice to eat the fruit from the Tree of Knowledge is framed as the moment humanity "fell from grace." But that framing is patriarchal interpretation—not divine truth.

Most people accepted this oppressive assertion as truth just because they have read it in a text.

Eve is not the villain, she's the portal. She is the embodiment of divine curiosity, sacred knowledge, and feminine awakening. Without her we would be in a static and fixed state without the freedom to flow.

The Sanhedrin, as the Jewish ruling council during the Second Temple period, did not literally write the Bible, but they shaped and curated the religious texts, heavily influencing which stories were preserved, emphasized, or excluded. Later, early Christian church fathers continued this pattern—editing, translating, and canonizing the Bible through patriarchal and political lenses.

The Bible was written, compiled, and edited almost entirely by men in positions of religious authority.
Women's voices, mystical traditions, and feminine expressions of the divine were either suppressed or left out entirely.

Books that honored feminine power, sensuality, or direct communion with the Divine were left out of the canon.

The Gospel of Mary (Magdalene): Shows her as a spiritual leader and confidant of Jesus was excluded.

The Book of Enoch and others with mystical teachings were also excluded or buried.

Anything that connects humankind to their true identity as co-creators with the universe and self governing was suppressed in an attempt to maintain patriarchal leadership. Just refer to today's political leadership and watch it played out in real time right before your eyes.

Patriarchy has long understood that controlling knowledge and truth is essential to maintaining power. Across centuries, it has strategically erased or distorted spiritual and historical truths in books, classrooms, and broader education systems to ensure that narratives supporting feminine power, indigenous wisdom, and holistic worldviews remain marginalized or forgotten. This erasure is not accidental; it is a calculated effort to shape collective memory and identity in ways that uphold hierarchical, male-centered dominance.

The classroom becomes one of patriarchy's most effective tools in this cultural erasure. Students are taught a history that is linear, male-centered, and sanitized, rarely encountering the rich spiritual traditions that honored the interconnectedness of life. The great library of Alexandria, which housed countless sacred texts including those celebrating feminine wisdom, was destroyed as an early and violent symbol of how patriarchy treats knowledge it cannot control. Today, bans on certain books, the whitewashing of history, and the marginalization of non-Western philosophies continue this legacy, ensuring that generations grow up disconnected from deeper truths about their heritage and their spiritual potential.

Spiritual and historical truth wasn't erased, it was just buried. And now many are rising to reclaim it not to destroy faith, but to restore balance, reawaken divine feminine wisdom, and rewrite the story with truth, love, and power.

Disconnection from Feminine Wisdom

Mitochondrial Eve: The Mother of Us All

Mitochondrial Eve represents the Divine Mother Lineage, the unbroken feminine transmission of wisdom, life force, and sacred memory encoded in our cells. Long before history was written in books, it was encoded in blood. Before the names of empires and kings were carved into stone, there was a woman unknown by name, but unforgettable in legacy. She lived in Africa over 150,000 years ago. Science calls her Mitochondrial Eve. Not necessarily the Eve of biblical legend, but the matrilineal ancestor from whom all living humans today descend. Not the first woman, but the most recent common mother of us all. You do the math. I believe that she is the Eve of ancient history's descendant.

This is not mythology, it is mitochondrial truth.

Mitochondrial Eve is the most recent woman whose mitochondrial DNA (mtDNA) has been passed down through an unbroken line of mothers to every living human being today.

Mitochondria, the tiny powerhouses within our cells, carry a small bit of DNA that is inherited only from the mother. This means our mitochondrial lineage follows a sacred, uninterrupted maternal thread.

Through studying mtDNA in people across the globe, geneticists traced our common maternal line back to one woman who lived in East Africa roughly 150,000 to 200,000 years ago. She is not the only woman who lived at that time—but all other maternal lines eventually faded. Hers endured.

The Divine Feminine in Our DNA

Mitochondrial Eve reminds us that we are all connected through the motherline. Every breath, every heartbeat, every step we take is powered by the cellular energy passed down from her womb to ours.

This is not just biology. It is an ancestral memory.

She carried the blueprint of life not only in her body, but in her Sacred Feminine wisdom. Her mitochondrial spark—passed from womb to womb—was carried through generations of mothers, midwives, warriors, farmers, artists, healers, enslaved women, and freedom seekers... all the way to you.

In her, we find a mirror of the primordial feminine, the divine energy that births not just children, but nations, languages, and songs.

Mitochondrial Eve lived in Africa, affirming what scientists have now confirmed: humanity began on the continent of Black women. The original mother was a Black woman. This truth shatters borders, racisms, and imagined hierarchies. It humbles the empire. It makes kin of strangers.

Henrietta Lacks (1920–1951) was an African American woman whose cancer cells were taken without her knowledge or consent during treatment for cervical cancer at Johns Hopkins Hospital in 1951. These cells, now known as HeLa cells, became the first immortal human cell line. They could survive and reproduce indefinitely in lab conditions, which was a scientific breakthrough.

Why Henrietta Lacks matters:

- **Medical Breakthroughs:**
  HeLa cells helped in developing the polio vaccine, cancer research, AIDS research, gene mapping, IVF (in vitro fertilization), and countless other medical advancements.
- **Ethical Issues:**
  Neither Henrietta nor her family were informed that her cells were being used. For decades, her descendants were also left in the dark, even as her cells generated profits for biotech companies and fueled major scientific achievements.

In a world so quick to divide, her existence calls us back to the source and to the one womb we all once passed through. The implications are radical: to dishonor any woman is to dishonor the lineage we all share.

Objectification is just as much of a devastating blow to the disruption of Sacred Feminine Energy as emotional and anthropological suppression in its effort to maintain power structures.

When women are seen as objects rather than autonomous beings, it becomes easier to justify denying them rights, roles, leadership, and voice. Objectification is the first step to dehumanization and control.

The Sacred Feminine is wildly intuitive, deeply feeling, and deeply knowing. She threatens patriarchal systems with her wisdom, sensuality, and refusal to be tamed. Objectifying her flattens that power into a palatable, commodified version.

Women's bodies are often marketed as products—to sell things, to symbolize success, to gratify the male ego. Media and culture perpetuate this because it feeds industries and insecurities alike.

The objectification of women under distorted masculine traits enforces unattainable beauty standards, which can lead to body dysmorphia, eating disorders, low self-worth, codependency, and other symptomatic dis-eases. The beauty industry thrives on this behavior, selling products that are scientifically proven to disrupt hormonal balance and cause health disparities in women globally.

Media and cultural narratives often portray women as rivals, especially in contexts related to beauty, relationships, and success. Such portrayals perpetuate stereotypes and influence real-life interactions among women. When women compete against each other, they operate in a toxic masculine mindset and miss opportunities to nurture and provide the necessary support needed for entire communities to thrive.

The toxic emotional and psychological impact of patriarchal imbalance affects women, children, families and communities at large. The pressure to prove worth through achievement, instead of being valued for who you are, leads to exhaustion and disconnection from feminine truth and compassion.

While on vacation in Mexico, I met Mia and Mark. It would seem that my own relationship trauma must have caused them to be energetically drawn to me. Like myself, Mia was an unseen partner in a competitive marriage.

Mia married Mark, a successful entrepreneur, who believed in the "traditional" roles of men and women. His career was his world, and Mia was expected to support him in every way—running the household, taking care of the children, and providing emotional support. Mia's worth was always tied to Mark's success. She was told that being a "good wife" meant being silent and supportive of his career. However, Mark never acknowledged how much Mia sacrificed for him to reach his ambitions. She had given up her own career and dreams to raise the children and support his work, and yet, every time she expressed dissatisfaction, she was reminded that her purpose was to serve him. Mia found herself proving her worth to her husband every day, sacrificing her individuality and aspirations for a man who never fully saw or valued her as a person outside of his success.

Many women can identify with Mia. When a husband doesn't honor or add to your energetic treasure chest by acknowledging and appreciating you, you find yourself feeling frustrated, hopeless, empty and alone. Emotional negligence and abuse is an epidemic in the world, but goes unrecognized because there are no external wounds.

Emotional neglect happens when one partner is emotionally unavailable, dismisses or ignores the other's needs, or fails to provide care, affection, and support. It can lead to feelings of loneliness, frustration, and insecurity, as one partner feels invisible or unimportant in the relationship. Women are sometimes mocked by other women for giving voice to their pain. If you've never experienced it yourself, you couldn't begin to understand. The behavior becomes normalized and women accept it and live with it.

The Collective Disconnect: When Survival Becomes Our Ground State

When survival becomes the ground state for a collective, something profound shifts in the human spirit. The body, mind, and soul become locked in a state of constant tension, where the focus is merely on getting by—not thriving, not growing, not healing. The essence of life becomes distorted as the pursuit of mere existence takes precedence over all else.

There is a shift taking place in the universe. Humankind has suffered under the dominant rule of toxic masculine leadership. This energy is generated from the egoic realm where resources for survival are perceived as scarce. The ego is vital to human survival, but without the understanding of the life-giving and sustaining power of the feminine realm, survival becomes our ground state, preventing us from realizing the abundance built into all of creation.

When survival is a daily necessity, stress and fear dominate. Fight or flight becomes the natural state. There is no room for peace, for play, or growth, only for endurance. People become disconnected from their own deeper truths because the mind is too focused on immediate threats, whether financial, emotional, or physical.

We live in a world where overbearing masculine leadership has disconnected humanity from its own internal governance, its sacred operating system. As individuals, we have outsourced our autonomy to systems that exist outside of us. We have exchanged (OI), organic intelligence for (AI), artificial intelligence. Make that make sense in the scheme of the universe.

In Ayurveda, an ancient healing system, health is not just the absence of disease but a state of wholeness—where body, mind, and spirit are in harmony. Emotions, when

fully experienced and understood, lead us back to this
state.

People are feeling the full weight of oppression,
greed-imposed lack, and despair created by patriarchal
values rooted in material acquisition, power over others,
and a scarcity mindset. Humanity is hardwired for survival,
but we are created to thrive.

Toxic masculinity celebrates domination and conquest,
gorging itself on the natural resources that Mother Earth
provides freely. What kind of dis-ease blinds men from
unconditional love, consideration, and abundance? Only
the disease of a hardened heart and an uncultivated mind.

As my grandmother once said, "They've got just enough
brains to be dangerous." Intellect and ego have their place,
but they must be integrated with consciousness—our
ground state.

Many are seeking respite but don't know where to find it.
Some turn to substances and distractions that temporarily
soothe but eventually compound emotional, financial, and
spiritual distress. Society tells you that your value lies
outside of you. But the truth is, your sacred essence is
within.

The Imprint of Patriarchy: Identity, Media, and Misalignment

From the time you are born, your identity has been shaped
by exogenous forces. Most people have never had an
original thought—they live in programs, following
narratives crafted to control.

The mass media "broadcasts" spells through words and
images that control how we should think, feel, and be. This
programming disconnects us from our intuitive knowing
and emotional equity.

In today's hyper-connected world, the media has become a powerful mirror—reflecting and shaping how people see themselves and others. From television shows and films to advertisements and social media, the messages we consume daily are steeped in cultural values. Among the most pervasive of these values are patriarchy and toxic masculinity.

Through the media, patriarchy and toxic masculinity silently script how people are expected to behave, feel, and relate to one another—often with harmful consequences.

At the core of patriarchy is the belief that men should hold power and dominance in all spheres of life, from politics to family dynamics. This belief is heavily reinforced in media portrayals, where men are frequently cast as strong, stoic, and in control, while women are shown as passive, emotional, or primarily valued for their physical appearance. These roles may seem like mere storytelling, but they deeply influence how individuals understand themselves and they perpetuate masculine and feminine imbalance.

Toxic masculinity is a byproduct of patriarchy and it emerges when traditional male norms are taken to an extreme. It encourages emotional repression, aggression, dominance, and the rejection of anything perceived as "feminine," producing monsters that unleash their venom on adults and innocent children.

The media plays a significant role in promoting these ideals. Male characters who express emotions, seek help, or show compassion are often portrayed as weak or laughable. Meanwhile, violence, sexual conquest, and control are depicted as signs of strength. This not only shapes male identity in damaging ways but also sets a dangerous standard for how men are expected to behave in relationships, workplaces, and society at large.

Two powerful and recent examples are Sean "Diddy" Combs. For decades, Diddy has been seen as a symbol of Black male success—wealthy, powerful, stylish, untouchable. But behind the image, recent footage of him physically assaulting singer Cassie Ventura has surfaced, triggering national conversations around abuse, image, and masculinity. Diddy's public persona was built on the media's celebration of dominance: over business, over culture, over women. He embodied what patriarchy teaches men to aspire to, control and power at all costs.

Donald Trump built a public brand around dominance, wealth, and a "tough guy" persona. His history of degrading comments about women and the infamous Access Hollywood tape, where he bragged about sexual assault, reflect toxic masculinity in action. Despite this, he gained and maintained massive support, showing how toxic male behavior can be excused, or even admired when it aligns with patriarchal power.

When women speak up about abuse, discrimination, or inequality, they are often questioned, doubted, or dismissed. Women are often asked, "Why didn't you leave?" instead of, "Why did he abuse her?" Women are taught to endure, to fix men, or to "ride or die", making them feel that suffering is part of love. This can cause long-term trauma, not just from the abuse itself but from believing it was normal or deserved.

Our society is suffering from collective dis-ease. Statistics affirm what our souls already know. When women are socialized to suppress, endure, and serve within a system that devalues their voices and bodies, it doesn't just affect their emotions—it affects their entire well-being by causing stress. Stress is one of the most common and damaging ways patriarchy and toxic masculinity affect women's health especially because it's often invisible and normalized.

Chronic stress activates the fight-or-flight response, keeping the body in a constant state of alert. Over time, this leads to:

- High blood pressure
- Elevated cortisol levels, which can cause weight gain and fatigue
- Disrupted sleep cycles
- Digestive problems and IBS
- Hormonal imbalances (impacting periods, fertility, libido, etc.)
- Weakened immune system
- Hair loss, acne, and skin issues
- Women who experience severe stress have a 45% increased risk of developing heart disease. (American Heart Association)
- Gender biases in healthcare often lead to misdiagnosis or inadequate treatment. Women are 50% more likely than men to be misdiagnosed following a heart attack. (Journal of the American Heart Association)

Why, in a world of abundance, are we surrounded by suffering? Systemic imbalance is the culprit. As above, so below and as within, so without. The entire universe is a reflection, a mirror.

The same way our bodies get sick from imbalance, so do our homes, communities, and our environment. Patriarchal systems ignore the rhythms and wisdom of the Sacred Feminine—and until we return to her, we will remain unwell.

We normalize sickness and disease. Folks are decaying all around us from stress and imbalance and we are shocked when we hear that another loved one, friend or coworker has lost their life. Society doesn't value wellbeing judging by what is allowed to pass as nutrition, the way that work-life balance is theorized, but not prioritized, and how the ease of Sacred Feminine is devalued in favor of the hardship of toxic masculinity.

Transformation Through Sacred Feminine Wisdom

Sacred Affirmation: "I recognize imbalance in my life and take steps to restore harmony."

Sacred Feminine Practice: Breathwork for regulating hormones, relieving stress, and restoring balance. The vagus nerve regulates your stress response. Deep breathing exercises conditions and tones the vagus nerve allowing you to stay more relaxed when encountering stress from the fight-or-flight response and the release of cortisol, the stress hormone. Breathe deeply into your belly for 4 counts, hold for 7 counts while being mindful of your breath filling your belly. Then, breathe out slowly for a count of 8 while noticing your breath being released from your belly. Do this cycle 10 times slowly and notice how you feel.

Sacred Reflection: Where have I internalized patriarchal values, and how can I shift toward a more balanced perspective? Do you favor competition over autonomy? Do you lack compassion? Do you neglect wellness habits and prioritize hard work? Do you use force and manipulation in your interactions with others in order to reach your goals?

Sacred Prayer: I have the power to heal. I am available to receive new information and build a new mindset. I attract those experiences that support my transformation and I detach my thoughts and actions from past experiences that do not serve my highest purpose as a sacred feminine being. I declare these abilities as my birthright and divine design.

Chapter 4:

Signs of Suppressed Feminine Energy

The Role of the Sacred Masculine

A key role of the Sacred Masculine is to encourage the growth and flourishing of the Sacred Feminine. The Sacred Masculine understands the value of balance and partnership, and supports the feminine energy by making space for her to rise, thrive, and reclaim her power.

Fathers shape their daughters' sense of value through how they honor the Sacred Feminine in everyday life. A balanced masculine presence displays protective, supportive, and emotionally intelligent behaviors toward women, modeling healthy interactions for future generations. When the Sacred Masculine celebrates a woman's intuition, creativity, and nurturing power, it affirms her divine design. The Sacred Masculine is not domineering, it is a joyful provider and a conscientious protector.

The Burden of Imbalance: Why Women Are Forced to Rely on Masculine Energy in the Absence of Fathers and Sacred Masculine Partners

In the delicate dance of life, feminine and masculine energies are meant to exist in harmony, complementing each other in balance and purpose. However, in many modern households and relationships, women are increasingly forced to rely on their masculine energy to survive, lead, and protect themselves and their families. This imbalance often begins in childhood with the absence of a father and is perpetuated in adulthood when husbands or partners fail to embody the Sacred Masculine. The consequence is a generation of women burdened by responsibilities that were never meant to be carried alone.

The Father Wound: A Disrupted Foundation

A father's presence in a daughter's life is often the first introduction to masculine energy. A father who is loving, present, and protective offers emotional security, guidance, and a model for how healthy masculine energy supports and nurtures the feminine. When a father is absent whether physically, emotionally, or spiritually, a void forms. Girls often internalize this absence as abandonment, unworthiness, or the message that masculine support is unreliable or unavailable.

Many girls were taught either to fear boys or surrender to their authority. The idea that boys always triumph in society while indiscriminately plucking one flower and then another from the proverbial garden filled me with disdain. My mother downloaded messages that were communicated out of fear and her desire to protect me in the absence of a father. The information was correct, but the energy lacked the proper frequency necessary for me to embrace it in a powerful, and most purposeful way. Instead of feeling empowered, I felt like a victim.

A father's love, presence, and emotional example can deeply influence a girl's ability to form healthy, loving relationships with boys (and others) throughout her life.

When a father treats his daughter and her mother with consistency, patience, and respect, he sets the standard. She learns what it feels like to be honored, heard, and valued. That becomes her baseline, not a bonus.

She won't mistake attention for affection, or control for love, because she knows what real care looks like.

I didn't have my father in the home and did not even believe that I missed having one until I started practicing journaling, meditation and self-reflection.

My father's absence was as a result of separation, divorce and a well meaning effort on my mother's part to protect me from my own father. Now I look back on my life and realize that, when a father has an opportunity to tell his daughter she's beautiful, smart, and worthy—not because of what she does, but because of who she is, he helps build unshakable self-esteem. That deep sense of being "enough" shields her from settling for less in all aspects of her life.

When a father is emotionally present and able to say, "I love you," able to apologize, able to express vulnerability—he teaches his daughter that masculinity and sensitivity can coexist. This shapes what she'll expect emotionally from future partners.

As girls grow into women, they may unconsciously begin to compensate for that void. To protect themselves, they develop traits like assertiveness, independence, hyper-vigilance, and control all expressions of masculine energy. These qualities are often praised in professional settings, yet when rooted in survival rather than balance, they can become burdensome. The feminine creative, intuitive, nurturer is suppressed in favor of the masculine in order to feel safe and in control.

Girls who feel seen by their fathers, or even their mothers are less likely to receive unhealthy validation from boys. Mothers who understand the need to validate their daughters won't prepare them to relate to males from a place of inferiority or fear, but from a place of self-awareness and autonomy, boundaries and soft power.

The Partner Gap: When Men Don't Embody the Sacred Masculine

Marriage or committed partnership is an opportunity to heal or reinforce patterns formed in childhood. Unfortunately, many women find themselves partnered with men who have not matured into the Sacred Masculine. The Sacred Masculine is strong yet gentle, firm yet empathetic. He leads without dominating, protects without controlling, and creates space for the feminine to flourish without fear.

In modern society, many men are disconnected from this sacred role. They may be emotionally unavailable, spiritually immature, or stuck in toxic masculine ideals such as domination, aggression, or detachment. This forces their partners into positions of leadership, decision-making, and emotional labor tasks that require the activation of masculine energy.

Rather than being held and supported, women become the holders and supporters. Rather than being cherished, they must be the protectors. Rather than flowing in their feminine softness, they are required to armor up and "do it all." Never revealing the chink in their armor.

Masculinity is often worn as a mask to hide emotional imbalance and brokenness. I've experienced this in my own life and have witnessed it at every turn. Work is a welcomed refuge in exchange for emotional negligence for the underdeveloped masculine energy. Patriarchy has made the gift of "work" an immutable quality to prove a worthiness. A woman could have a husband, children and a career and function as a single parent because he "works." Her work is less valuable. His work provides him status. Having a family also provides him status and a level of respectability. Corporate firms often select candidates for partnership that are typically married men that have, or plan to have children while simultaneously requiring them to work long hours neglecting those families.

The High Cost of Imbalance

Living primarily in masculine energy may bring success in the external world, but it often comes at the cost of internal peace. Women become exhausted, disconnected from their intuition, and hardened by the need to constantly self-protect. Their bodies suffer from hormonal imbalances to chronic fatigue. Their relationships suffer from power struggles to emotional distance. Their spirits suffer from feeling unseen, unsupported, and deeply alone.

The Invitation for Healing and Wholeness

The healing begins with acknowledgment. Recognizing the patterns that come from father wounds and unbalanced partnerships is the first step. Women can begin the journey back to their femininity by creating safe inner and outer environments where softness is not punished but honored. And men, too, must rise reclaiming the Sacred Masculine within themselves, healing their own wounds, and stepping into their divine roles as protectors, providers, and conscious partners.

True balance comes not from one energy dominating the other, but from mutual respect, reverence, and co-creation. When the Sacred Masculine returns, the Sacred Feminine can finally rest and rise in her full glory.

Diagnosing the Root Cause: Generational Suppression of the Feminine Energy

We are not only women, we are creators of all life both physically and metaphysically. We are mothers that carry the divine flame of life and grandmothers of sacred evolution.

Generational suppression of sacred energy lives in the body as stored toxic energy, or trauma. Science now recognizes that trauma can be stored in the body and passed down through epigenetics, meaning that the emotional and psychological wounds of our ancestors can alter our genetic expression.

These toxic energies are passed down through behaviors, beliefs, and emotional imprints. Women have carried wounds of silence, suppression, and survival for centuries

These inherited patterns show up as:

- Hyper-independence or codependency
- Fear of vulnerability or rejection of feminine softness
- Chronic self-sacrifice and emotional suppression
- Attraction to emotionally unavailable partners
- Internalized beliefs that worth is earned through service or suffering

Our foremothers were taught to endure; our mothers were taught to perform. Now we are awakening to transmute and transform alchemically, and write new genetic codes that cultivate soft power.

Endurance was survival. For Black women, Indigenous women, and women across the globe, endurance was not a choice—it was a lifeline. My foremothers were women in the rural south raising children while working in the fields or serving in white households. They held their grief quietly, swallowed their rage, and prayed in whispers as their children and partners were sold or slaughtered as chattel. Her softness was a luxury she could not afford.

Prayer circles, quilting, singing spirituals, braiding hair—each was an act of resistance, a coded language of survival passed from woman to woman. They didn't speak of healing, they were the root that held the family tree together. Their strength was often unrecognized, but it built nations.

Our Mothers Were Taught to Perform

The next generation learned to be twice as good to get half as far. They polished their pain into a presentation. They chased excellence, but often at the expense of emotional rest.

They dressed perfectly, smiled constantly, and hid their exhaustion behind productivity. They were the image of success, but at night, their souls were weary.

Our mothers broke ceilings—but sometimes they were also broken. They gave us access. They taught us discipline. But many longed for a softer, more authentic way of being.

We Are Awakening to Transformation

Now, a new wave of Sacred Feminine energy is rising. We are choosing to transform. We are healing ancestral wounds, unlearning grind culture, and returning to sacred balance.

Women are leaving their run of the mill, 9-to-5 jobs to become doulas, herbalists, or spiritual teachers, not because it's easy, but because it's aligned. They now rest without guilt, cry without shame. They make room for joy and outrage. They are reclaiming "soft power"!

The Cost of Misunderstood Femininity

When patriarchal oppression was at its highest, particularly during slavery, colonization, and the height of Jim Crow and segregation, Black women bore an incredibly heavy and complex burden, yet they also embodied some of the most profound resilience, creativity, and spiritual power the world has ever seen.

Black women endured the brutal force of white supremacy and patriarchy simultaneously. They were:

- Sexually exploited and dehumanized. Enslaved Black women were seen as property, breeders, and laborers.
- Denied womanhood in contrast to the pedestal of "true womanhood" reserved for white women. Black women were denied softness, protection, and rest.
- Expected to labor endlessly in the fields, in white homes, and within their own families, often with no reprieve or recognition.

Despite all this, Black women:

- Kept ancestral wisdom alive through food, stories, healing practices, music, and spirituality.
- Built networks of care for one another and for entire communities, often becoming the emotional, spiritual, and practical backbone of resistance.
- Raised generations under unimaginable pressure, teaching children dignity, faith, and strength in the face of injustice.

Throughout history, Black women have stood at the crossroads of oppression and resilience, often tasked with the sacred yet heavy responsibility of raising generations while bearing the weight of societal injustice, economic disparity, and cultural erasure. From slavery to systemic racism, through single motherhood, to the frontlines of civil rights movements, Black women have been both the nurturers and the warriors quietly cultivating strength in the soil of adversity.

Harriet Tubman, who escaped slavery yet returned repeatedly to free others, becoming a living embodiment of courage and maternal instinct. Though she had no biological children of her own, her protective love extended to dozens of people she called family. Her life teaches us that motherhood is not only a biological calling but a spiritual one—rooted in a commitment to nurture, guide, and liberate.

Fannie Lou Hamer, born into a family of sharecroppers, turned her pain into purpose. Sterilized without her consent, she was denied the opportunity to bear children of her own, yet she helped raise nieces, nephews, and entire communities. She stood boldly against the violence of racism while planting seeds of freedom through education, food co-ops, and grassroots leadership. Under unimaginable pressure, she chose to rise, to mother a movement.

Michelle Obama carried the ancestral weight of Black womanhood with elegance and intentionality. As First Lady, she nurtured her daughters and a nation, amplifying health, education, and the value of authenticity. Behind the global spotlight was a woman deeply rooted in her mother's strength, her community's values, and the quiet fortitude of those who came before her.

Countless Black grandmothers, aunties, and mothers worked multiple jobs, sat in pews on Sundays, and carried whole households on their backs. They held space for healing when the world gave no shelter. Their kitchens became temples. Their words became scripture. Their endurance became inheritance.

- Spiritual Resistance: Through African-rooted spiritual systems, prayer, conjure, and church leadership, Black women created channels of empowerment that helped them reclaim their humanity.
- Cultural Resistance: In hair, dress, and song, Black women expressed defiance, beauty, and sovereignty.
- Political Resistance: From Harriet Tubman to Sojourner Truth, Ida B. Wells to Fannie Lou Hamer, Black women were often the unseen strategists and boldest truth-tellers in freedom movements.

What unites all these women is not merely survival, but sacred intention. They did not raise children solely to endure the world, but to change it. They passed down not only lessons but legacies forged in dignity, sacrifice, and divine intuition. The inner voice that guided them was not always audible, but it was clear: Protect, provide, persist, prevail.

Unseen Emotional Labor

Even within Black communities, patriarchy showed up often silencing Black women's voices or burdening them with the weight of everyone's healing but their own. Yet still, they led with heart-centered wisdom while holding sacred grief and still embodied joy and created spaces for liberation through mothering, teaching, organizing, and spiritual leadership.

Today, we stand on the shoulders of their devotion. Every generation touched by their love is proof that even under unimaginable pressure, Black women do not simply hold up the world, they raise it.

The Sacred Feminine Never Died

Even under oppression, Black women remained living vessels of the Sacred Feminine nurturers, seers, healers, midwives, priestesses in disguise. Their power wasn't always recognized, but it was real, ancestral, and transformative. They often had to transmute the pain brought into their homes by husbands after they were disrespected and dehumanized, only to come home and exact the same toxic energy onto their own wives and children.

Our feminine power has been filtered through masculine lens. What is intuitive has been labeled irrational. What is soft has been called weak. Emotional expression has been dismissed as hysteria.

Feminine energy favors rest, nurturing, empathy, and collaboration. It is created through inspired action not striving. It is the source of life, not just through childbirth, but through creative ideas, healing, and transformation. Feminine power cannot be measured in volume or force, because it is the essence of divine flow.

From Cultural Programming to Divine Identity

Most women have been subconsciously programmed to diminish themselves from a young age. Cultural myths, media messages, and religious traditions often teach conformity, silence, and self-denial.

The family is the first classroom where power is taught.

When that power is disconnected from love, generations suffer.

In the American South, white women raised under the "Southern Belle" ideal were often trained to be delicate, submissive, and emotionally silent—seen but not heard. They married men who expected obedience, not partnership. Sons were taught to dominate. Daughters were taught to shrink.

Behind the grand plantations and lace gloves were women suffering from depression, addiction, and loneliness, unable to express the full range of their humanity.

But when balance is restored and when the masculine protects rather than controls, and the feminine is honored rather than silenced, healing becomes not only possible but inevitable.

A divinely feminine woman learns to maintain emotional balance by practicing physical and emotional wellness. Ayurveda teaches that all life experiences are internalized and emotions must be digested just like the food that we eat. Nutrition isn't just what we eat, but what we can digest. The mouth is the gateway to nutrition through digestion and the pathway that carries thoughts on a journey from our hearts and minds out into the manifested material world. Thoughts become things. Likewise we must guard our emotional gates: our eyes, ears, hearts, and minds. They are gateways to our sacred state of being.

You were never meant to be molded by exterior opinions, you were meant to be self-aware, autonomous, self-governing and transformative. The truth is, your body is a temple, divinely intertwined with the source of your being and every other thing that divine, life-force energy has created.

It's a laboratory where you process and alchemize experiences transforming undesirable ones from darkness into light, and metal into gold with sacred practices.

Signs of Inherited Trauma & Spiritual Suppression

In many lineages, feminine wisdom was erased or demonized. Women were taught to disconnect from their intuition, avoid spiritual practices, and obey external authorities. In doing so, generations lost access to inner knowing, rituals, and sacred emotional expression.

Symptoms of inherited trauma may include:

- People-pleasing and perfectionism
- Suppressed anger or sadness
- Shame around self-care, sexuality, or emotional needs
- Self-sacrifice and being taken for granted

We are meant to evolve and heal from diseases our ancestors could not resolve rather than repeating and perpetuating them. We come into this experience to form new evolutionary pathways by transforming, transmuting and alchemizing self-limiting thoughts, beliefs and experiences into pure gold.

We must tell a new story of becoming the sacred co-creators who through balanced emotions, intuition, creativity and inspired actions, invite frequencies of collaboration, acceptance, and equality as stewardship to both our creator and Mother Earth.

The Return to Sacred Practices

Restoring your Sacred Feminine power requires daily ritual and spiritual nourishment. Practices like:

- Meditation and breathwork
- Journaling and emotional witnessing
- Dance, movement, and creative expression
- Moon rituals, energy healing, prayer

These practices reconnect you to your ground state, your natural vibration of conscious awareness and peace. In Ayurveda, this state is called "homeostasis", a holistic state of equilibrium where mind, body, and spirit move in harmony.

Emotional Wisdom as Sacred Guidance

Emotions are not weaknesses; they are sacred messengers.

- Fear invites trust
- Anger invites boundaries
- Sadness invites release

Feminine energy doesn't suppress emotion—it partners with it in a sacred, sensual dance of pleasure and pain. It understands that joy doesn't mean the absence of suffering, but is the pathway to wholeness.

The late author, Toni Morrison used storytelling as medicine for the soul.

Toni Morrison didn't just write novels, she conjured ancestral memory. Her work, *Beloved and The Bluest Eye*, came from deep within the womb of the collective Black feminine experience. She wrote from feeling, from spirit, from an inner knowing that honored the pain, beauty, and resilience of womanhood. Her characters often navigated trauma, but Morrison never exploited them, she held them with tenderness, offering the reader transformation rather than spectacle.

The Power of Ground State and Energetic Harmony

As we've discussed, everything in existence is composed of energy, and energy naturally seeks harmony and balance. The ground state represents the most stable, natural, and effortless energetic condition—where energy is not forced or scattered but in its most aligned and restful form.

Every thought, feeling, and choice affects your body's chemistry. Your hormonal and emotional balance, sacred rhythm and flow, and mindfulness, support your state of being—your ground state of conscious awareness.

In physics, the ground state is the lowest energy state of a system, meaning it is in its most stable and natural form. From a spiritual and energetic perspective, this corresponds to:

- A state of deep inner peace (not overly excited or depleted).
- Energetic alignment with the present moment (not resisting or forcing outcomes).
- Being fully grounded in the body and soul's true essence (free from external distortions or conditioning).

The ground state is where manifestation flows easily, and energy is not wasted in unnecessary struggle. It is the seat of Sacred Feminine power, allowing one to attract rather than chase, to be, rather than force.

In Ayurveda, the ground state is not something you must achieve, it is your original, natural state. Disease, stress, and imbalance occur when we become separated from it.

The Sacred Feminine honors this. She doesn't labor for healing; she accesses it through ease, grace and self-awareness. She becomes the constant gardener of her own heart and soul, cultivating wholeness with daily rituals and intention.

Transformation Through Sacred Feminine Wisdom

Sacred Affirmation: "I release what no longer serves me with gratitude and grace. I honor my body as a sacred vessel of wisdom and beauty."

Sacred Feminine Practice: Sacred Movement (Dance or Sensual Flow)

Put on music that connects you to your soul and move freely. Let your hips lead. Feel every part of your body. Dance for yourself, not performance.

Sacred Reflection:

Release what I was taught to be,

And remember who I truly am.

Holy, whole, and worthy of devotion.

My body is a temple.

My heart is an altar.

My voice is a sacred drumbeat of truth.

Sacred Prayer:

Divine Mother within me, around me, before me,

I will return to you now.

To the softness that strengthens.

To the wisdom that whispers.

To the power that flows instead of forces.

PART III: GENERATIONAL TRANSFORMATION

(Transmuting Dis-ease and Inviting Wellness the Feminine Way)

Chapter 5:

Recognizing the Need for Cleansing and Renewal

(Inherited dis-ease and dysfunction: emotional, spiritual, relational)

When toxic emotions are not fully processed and continue to affect descendants, the trauma can be transmitted through learned behaviors, family dynamics, and even epigenetics, where stress alters gene expression, making future generations more vulnerable to anxiety, fear, emotional dysregulation and dis-ease.

Women who carry inherited trauma may struggle with feelings of unworthiness, fear, or grief that does not seem to have originated in their own life, but to mirror the survival responses of their ancestors that are locked deep within the DNA causing limited beliefs and potential.

Limiting beliefs are energetic imprints passed down through families, cultures, and societies, shaping how we see ourselves, our power, and our connection to the divine. Many of these beliefs stem from patriarchal conditioning, restricting the flow of Sacred Feminine energy and leading to emotional, physical, and spiritual dysfunction.

Common Limiting Beliefs That Suppress the Sacred Feminine

1. "I Must Be Small, Quiet, and Agreeable to Be Loved."

Root Cause: Generations of women were taught that being too opinionated, loud, or independent would result in rejection, punishment, or loss of love.

In society, being opinionated is taboo for women. Having your own mind and voicing your opinion is perceived as difficult and even mean spirited. I grew up an only child. I usually found myself the only child in a room full of adults. When someone had a party, adults requested my presence. I took coats at the door and taught my elders the latest dances. It was the seventies and the political climate and current events were brimming with conversational topics. I listened to all of the hot topics and was asked my thoughts and opinions. I was often told, " I'd been here before." I loved being acknowledged and included. It felt good to be acknowledged.

In adulthood, I express my feelings in relationships stating my boundaries or expressing my dissatisfaction in a romantic relationship. Expressions of my feelings were viewed as, "too emotional," or complaining and nagging.

Impact: Suppresses authentic self-expression (throat chakra blockage). Leads to people-pleasing, over-apologizing, and fear of taking up space, creating self-doubt and hesitation in pursuing desires and dreams.

2. "I Am Not Enough (or I Am Too Much)."

Root Cause: Women have been told they are either not enough (not strong, smart, or beautiful enough) or too much (too emotional, too sensitive, too ambitious).

Impact: Leads to low self-worth, imposter syndrome, and self-sabotage, creating a pattern of seeking external validation instead of trusting inner wisdom and disconnects women from their intuition and confidence.

The idea of not being enough is a deep wound. This wound is often formed in early childhood when natural self-expressions are met with judgement, neglect, or unrealistic expectations. It deepens as society projects unrealistic standards and expectations of beauty, productivity, and perfection onto women.

I decided early in life that it was important to create my own trends and standards. I discovered that it is impossible to please people. I was either too tall, too thin, too smart, too opinionated, or just too much! Creating my own image and being in control of my own narrative fills me with purpose and relieves me of external validation. I've learned to use the energy that I might have given over to others while being concerned about how I'm perceived by them to creative pursuits, spiritual worship, joy and contentment.

3. "My Worth Comes From Serving Others, Not Myself."

Root Cause: Women were conditioned to be caregivers, putting others' needs before their own.

Impact: Leads to burnout, exhaustion, and resentment, creating guilt around rest, pleasure, self-care and weakens personal boundaries, making it hard to say no.

From birth to death, women have long been the hands that soothe, heal, and uplift. Across cultures, classes, and communities, caregiving is most often seen as a natural extension of womanhood. Whether raising children, tending to aging parents, or nurturing entire communities. Women, particularly Black women, shoulder the sacred and often invisible labor of care. But this labor, while essential, comes at a cost.

My caregiving journey began when I was a child. I was delivered to my grandmother every morning. I went to elementary school only a block away from her home. After my grandmother had a heart attack, it became my responsibility to stay with her during the week night and some weekends just in case she had another emergency. I was only nine or ten, but I can still remember dreading going. My grandmother was an empath, loving, nurturing, but she could be a little scary and intimidating. I wasn't given a choice in the matter, so I accepted it. I learned a lot from my grandmother.

Childhood prepared me for the sacrifices of motherhood. I loved and cared for my children and family without the emotional support or nurturing energy of my partner.

I can remember asking him to pray with me for our family and was told that prayer was my responsibility.

As I shared earlier, women often provide the emotional heavy lifting patriarchal societies.

I know women who embrace the sole emotional burden as a martyr. Some even accept it as religious and cultural protocol quoting scripture to support their self-sacrifice without fully understanding its depth and breadth of the verses.

Everyone has a right to experience and understand life as they choose. Remember, you have the free will to create and attract life from wherever you resonate.

I watched my mom's health and wellbeing decline from the stress of caring for my stepfather. Although receiving hospice care at home, his needs far exceeded their scope of work. My mother cooked, bathed, picked him up when he'd fallen, and attended to his every discomfort. She was in her nineties, and although she admitted that it was too much for her, she persevered against my advice because she felt it was her duty to sacrifice her wellbeing for that of her husband.

Now, I have moved home to care for her. Caring for my stepfather has taken a heavy toll on her life. We are taught to wear sacrifice as a badge of honor, but who's there for us when we become depleted.

4. "Rest and Pleasure Are Selfish."

Root Cause: Patriarchy glorifies hustle culture and self-sacrifice, making rest and pleasure seem lazy or indulgent.

Impact: Causes chronic stress, adrenal fatigue, and hormonal imbalances and disconnects women from their sensuality, creativity, and joy, creating guilt when choosing ease over struggle.

The idea of rest and quality sleep is lost on women in patriarchal societies. We are constantly expressing our fatigue and need for rest, but rarely intentionally allow it for ourselves. I can remember my mom often saying, "I don't /can't sleep during the day." Even when I find her napping today, she will deny it saying she's just watching television. I constantly find myself giving her permission to sleep.

5. "My Body Is Shameful or Needs to Be Controlled."

The control of women's reproductive systems is one of the most enduring expressions of patriarchy. From forced sterilizations to restricted access to birth control, from coerced childbirth to the criminalization of abortion, women have had to fight for the basic right to decide what happens within their own wombs.

Black, Indigenous, and other marginalized women have faced the worst of these violations. The forced sterilization of Black women in the U.S. South, Indigenous women in North America, and countless others across the globe is not just history, it is recent memory. Reproductive control has been used as a tool of colonization, racial oppression, and population control.

The foundation of reproductive rights for Black women in America is built upon a history of violence, control, and commodification. During their enslavement, Black women's reproductive autonomy was not just denied, it was weaponized. Their bodies became vessels for profit, their wombs viewed as property, and their children born into bondage.

Black women have been highly sexualized in the media by continuous programming that consistently awakens the generational codes that governed our womb when we were chattel for breeding. Honestly, this history is very emotionally triggering for me. I can feel its impact at the core of my being.

Understanding this history is essential to understanding the roots of reproductive injustice and the enduring legacy it has left on generations.

Root Cause: Generations of religious and cultural beliefs have labeled female bodies and sexuality as dangerous, impure, or sinful.

Impact: Leads to body dysmorphia, disordered eating, and sexual repression, creating womb and sacral chakra blockages, affecting fertility, menstrual health, and creativity and disconnects women from their sensual and divine power.

6. "I Must Work Harder to Prove My Worth."

Root Cause: Women have been told they must work twice as hard to be seen, valued, or respected.

Impact: Traps women in overworking, perfectionism, and burnout cycles blocking the ability to receive with ease and flow, creating deep fear of failure and difficulty asking for help.

I'm both proud and saddened by the conditions of educated, professional women. The responsibilities they are confronted with in today's society has forced many of them to lean into masculinity and abandon much of their Sacred Feminine energy. I have heard women compare their level of hard work with that of other women finding validation and pride in the ability to work to exhaustion and relish in self-sacrifice. That particular level of competition in work is usually reserved for masculinity. This shift isn't necessarily a betrayal of femininity, but an evolutionary survival strategy.

This masculinization of the feminine spirit is also reinforced in popular culture. The "strong independent woman" trope often celebrates toughness and self-reliance, but rarely makes space for vulnerability, rest, softness, or sacred femininity. Women are expected to "have it all"––career, family, flawless appearance but must never show signs of strain. To survive this demand, many armor themselves with a masculine shell.

7. "I Am Not Safe Being Seen or Heard."

Root Cause: Ancestral trauma from witch hunts, gender-based violence, and oppression has created a subconscious fear of being visible.

Impact: Leads to fear of speaking out, sharing wisdom, or taking up space, creating a pattern of hiding, playing small, or shrinking energy, causing anxiety, throat chakra blockages, and self-silencing.

There has been a long standing history of trauma inflicted on women who dared to embody the full spectrum of Sacred Feminine energy. Patriarchy has participated in the severing of a woman's connection to her own divine essence. At the core of this trauma is the belief that it is simply unsafe to exist fully in my truth.

Jealousy, envy and enmity exist deep within patriarchy for the Sacred Feminine. I have been described as a "gangster" by my spouse. In patriarchal societies, a woman who has her own voice is no longer in need of protection or provision. It seems that a woman must silence her voice and shrink, in order for men to feel the need to protect and provide for her.

Black women know all too well that they have historically had to speak up and even offer up their body as a sacrifice to save a brother, father, husband, or son from being lynched, or to keep her child from being sold. Now, we are considered the most unprotected class in society, because we have often been dishonored and abandoned by those we were compelled to protect.

Women Seek Refuge in Religious Institutions and Find Trauma

Spiritual trauma refers to the emotional, psychological, and existential pain caused by experiences that challenge or disrupt one's sense of connection to a higher power, purpose, or personal belief system. This trauma can arise from a variety of sources, often leaving individuals feeling disconnected from their spiritual identity, faith, or inner guidance. Here are some common causes and manifestations of spiritual trauma:

Religious Abuse or Manipulation

- Dogmatic Control: Experiences where spiritual teachings were used to control, shame, or manipulate

Spiritual Guilt

- Feeling condemned or unworthy due to beliefs about sin, failure, or spiritual inadequacy

Spiritual Disillusionment

- Realizing that certain spiritual practices or communities didn't align with your personal truth, leading to loss of spiritual growth.

When women begin sacred practices and denounce feminine suppression, powerful transformations often unfold personally, culturally, and spiritually.

Deep Inner Awakening

Sacred practices help women heal inherited trauma and internalized patriarchy. They start to release shame, guilt, and silence carried from mothers, grandmothers, and beyond—breaking cycles for the generations to come.

Reconnecting with their intuition, ancestral wisdom, and divine feminine energy will help women reconnect the divine spark. Sacred practices like meditation, womb healing, journaling, moon rituals, and prayer, open doorways to inner peace and power.

Reclaiming your Power

By transforming your thoughts and renewing your mind from programming that have historically suppressed your voice, body and intuitive wisdom, the Sacred Feminine can rise again.

You will experience the conscious awareness of your ground state and embrace autonomy, strengthen boundaries, realize self-worth as purpose, and feel the presence of soft power.

You will no longer invest your precious currency, energy or attention into systems that don't honor your Sacred Feminine capacity, or support your desire to collaborate and thrive.

The Beauty of Expression

Denouncing feminine suppression often births new creativity, self-expression, sensuality, and artistry. Women begin speaking truth, dressing to express themselves, and embodying their authenticity without apology.

There comes a time when the pain of staying the same overcomes the fear of change.

I've frequently heard mature women speak about finally reaching a stage in life when they care less about outward opinions and more about their own autonomy. For many, this phenomenon begins between forty and fifty. I can honestly attest to the fact that if I'd understood and embraced my Sacred Feminine journey to wholeness as a young woman, I would have enjoyed the benefits of "inner knowing" as a young woman, or maybe even in adolescence. Understanding my purpose, self-image and ability to attract healthy relationships of all kinds rests in my ability to sustain my ground state of conscious awareness. Being a witness to my own thoughts, feelings and experiences helps me constantly self-reflect. I do not give my precious currency of attention outwardly where there's little return on investment. I embrace a deep knowledge and understanding that I am a goddess and co-creator with the source of all that is.

My life is a canvas and I am an artist. It's like a movie and I write the script and choose the characters that will ultimately join me in my production and service in the material world. I imagine and then create the world in which I choose to live.

Community & Collective Awakening

As you rise individually, you will magnetize like-minded souls. Sacred sisterhoods will form, communities will grow, and new concepts are born. Together, women will amplify healing, empowerment, and justice on a global scale.

I proclaim, I Am Soft Power, as that community that will maintain and pass on the divine knowledge, practice and spark of Sacred Feminine energy through like minded and energetically aligned sisterhoods.

Embodiment of Sacred Feminine Guidance

Desmond Tutu, the South African Anglican bishop and social rights activist, often spoke about the importance and value of women in leadership roles. He believed that women bring unique and essential qualities to leadership, such as empathy, nurturing, and a collaborative approach. Tutu emphasized that these qualities are crucial for creating more just, peaceful, and equitable societies.

In his speeches and writings, Tutu highlighted the need for gender equality and the empowerment of women. He saw the inclusion of women in leadership as vital to addressing social injustices and fostering a more compassionate and inclusive world. Tutu's advocacy for women's leadership was rooted in his broader commitment to human rights and social justice.

One notable quote attributed to him on this topic is: "If we are going to see real development in the world then our best investment is women." This statement underscores his belief in the transformative power of women in leadership positions and their role in driving positive change.

In a 2019 event in Singapore, former President Barack Obama highlighted the positive impact of women's leadership on global issues. He remarked that if women were in charge of every country for two years, we would see significant improvements across various sectors. He stated, "There would be less war, kids would be better taken care of and there would be a general improvement in living standards and outcomes." (NPR.org)

I've deliberately chosen the word guidance over leadership, because I prefer the softer energetic frequency of the word guidance over the harder, more dominating energy of the historically patriarchal frequency of the term leadership. I believe that the bishop would agree.

In a world that often glorifies hierarchy, dominance, and control, the call for guidance over leadership emerges as a sacred rebalancing. This is not a rejection of leadership itself, but rather a transformation of what it means to lead, rooted in softness, presence, and soul.

Traditional leadership models tend to emphasize authority: one who stands at the front, making decisions, issuing directives, and being followed. This masculine-coded paradigm, while sometimes effective, can become rigid, hierarchical, and disconnected from the collective. In contrast, guidance flows from within and among, it listens before it speaks. It honors the wisdom in the room, not just the one holding the mic.

Guidance is the path of the healer, the teacher, the priestess, the elder. It doesn't demand attention; it invites trust. It does not command, but rather illuminates. The guide walks with you, not ahead of you. This approach honors the feminine principle as deeply intuitive, relational, and nurturing. It says: "I do not lead you away from yourself. I will help you return to your inner truth and wisdom."

When women reclaim Sacred Feminine energy and choose guidance over dominance, they become safe spaces for others to heal and build.

In this model, influence is not about visibility but about resonance. True guides are not attached to outcome or image; they are committed to presence, purpose, and mutual empowerment through collaboration.

As the world begins to heal from centuries of imbalance, guidance becomes not just preferable—it becomes evolutionary. It offers a new template: one where Sacred Feminine energy, listening, emotional intelligence, and shared wisdom lead the way.

Connection and Purpose

Healthy relationships and a sense of purpose are vital to long-term health. Love and service create coherence in the mind, body, and spirit.

A connected life is a healed life. Connection to self, to others, to nature, to Source is medicine. When we feel seen, safe, and soulfully aligned, the body relaxes. The heart opens. The nervous system softens. Healing becomes not just possible, but inevitable.

To live connected is to:

- listen deeply to your body's wisdom
- honor your emotions as sacred signals
- surround yourself with loving, reciprocal relationships
- remember you are part of something greater
- walk your path with purpose and presence

Disconnection from the ground state is the root of so much suffering. Connection is the return to wellness .

One of the hardest life lessons I have ever learned is how to distinguish and align with healthy, and productive relationships.

The foundation of all healthy relationships is self-awareness. The more you know your needs, values, and boundaries, the clearer it becomes who truly aligns with you and your highest self.

This is a lesson that every child should learn in their primary years. Self- awareness and emotional regulation go hand and hand.

Self-awareness is the sacred pause, the space where you observe what's happening within you before reacting to what's happening around you.

Life requires skill and relationships are where those skills are practiced and mastered. I'd always understood "life skills" as how to shop, cook, manage finances, pay your bills etc. These are skills that resonate in masculine prioritized systems, but life skills must include learning, self-awareness and self-regulation. Both of these skills have allowed me an opportunity to really get to know who I am, what I want and how to cultivate and protect both myself and my purpose.

Self-awareness is helping me notice what I'm feeling (emotionally and somatically), what core wounds or patterns are being activated and whether I'm engaging them from my authentic self or from old programming like fear and lack. Fear and lack is the worst place in which to form relationships. Fear of missing out, fear of time running out, fear of not having enough and fear of not being enough has often been an impediment in my life. Making choices from any of these places denied me of my true identity and landed me in relationships and circumstances that did not align with my highest most sacred self.

Transformation Through Sacred Feminine Wisdom

Sacred Affirmation: "My softness is my superpower. My presence is my prayer."

Sacred Feminine Practice: Carve out time weekly for silence and stillness. Let yourself receive rather than produce. Sit with a candle, journal, or simply your breath.

Sacred Reflection: I abide in the hope of a new day. Where in my body do I feel the most tension, and what does she need from me?

Sacred Prayer: Divine Mother within me, around me, before me, I return to your sacred well. Where stillness lives. Where softness breathes. Where I remember who I am. Let every part of me that has been silenced speak now with your voice, gentle but unshakable, tender but mighty.

Wrap me in your grace. Fill me with your wisdom. Let my intuition speak louder than fear, and my heart move freer than duty. I release the weight of roles that dim my light. I release the need to overprove, overdo, overgive. I choose rest. I choose ease. I choose to honor the goddess. I am becoming sacred. May I walk in beauty. May I speak in reverence. May I live as love.

PART IV:

The Sacred Cycles

Chapter 6:

Embracing the Sacred Feminine and Its Transformational Power

(Creation, Death, Burial, and Resurrection)

Across cultures and epochs, the pattern of birth, death, burial, and resurrection has served as the deepest metaphor for transformation. From the seed that must root in the earth before it sprouts, to the phoenix that rises from its own ashes, this cycle reminds us that endings are never final; they are invitations to a new becoming.

Every act of creation whether a birth of a child, a piece of art, or a new chapter in life begins with potential. In the fertile darkness of imagination or soil, a spark of life takes shape. This phase is filled with hope, vision, and the thrill of "what might be."

Just as fruit must fall from the tree, every created thing reaches its season of completion. Death isn't failure; it's the universe's way of clearing space. When we allow aspects of our lives, habits, relationships, and identities to die, we honor the natural flow of growth.

Burial is more than disposal; it's a ritual of reverence. When we consciously lay something to rest through ceremony, mourning, or ritual, we acknowledge its value and our grief. We give it back to the earth, where it becomes compost for the next cycle.

From that compost springs new life. Ideas germinate, relationships transform, and our own souls awaken to possibilities we couldn't have seen before. Resurrection isn't simply a return to what was; it's an evolution—something richer, wiser, and more aligned with our deepest truth.

I watched a documentary on regenerative farming. I find it amazing how everything reflects the oneness of creation.

Regenerative farming is more than a method of agriculture, it is a return to relationship. Rooted in reverence for the Earth, it honors the rhythms, intelligence, and cycles that mirror the Sacred Feminine herself. Where industrial farming extracts, dominates, and depletes, regenerative farming listens, nourishes, and restores. It is farming as a ceremony, where soil is sacred, and stewardship is spiritual.

At its core, regenerative farming focuses on healing. Healing the land, the ecosystem, and the farmer. It uses practices like cover cropping, composting, rotational grazing, and minimal tillage to bring life back to depleted soil. But beneath these techniques lies a deeper truth—it is the feminine principle of regeneration in action. Just as the womb renews life through cycles, the Earth renews herself when given space, care, and rest.

This practice is inherently collaborative. It acknowledges the interconnectedness of all beings—plants, animals, humans, and the unseen forces of nature. It teaches us that we are not above the Earth, but of her. That we must give back as much as we take, and perhaps even more. In this way, regenerative farming is not only about growing food; it is about growing wisdom, reciprocity, and balance.

In embracing regenerative farming, we embrace the Sacred Feminine—an energy that creates through harmony, not control. It invites us to remember that sustainability is not just a goal, but a way of being. One where every seed planted is an offering, and every harvest a blessing.

As women and those resonating in the frequency of Sacred Feminine energy rise to reclaim their inner knowing, we are also being called to remember our outer responsibilities as divine stewards of mother earth, as nurturers, as visionaries of a more balanced world. Regenerative farming offers us a blueprint—not just for agriculture, but for living. It invites us to reimagine economy, sustainability, and abundance through the lens of wholeness.

How Being a Plant Mother Helps Me Understand Death, Burial, and Resurrection

I am a plant mother. As a plant mother, I've come to see death not as an end, but as an essential part of becoming. Tending to the cycles of growth, decay, and bloom has taught me that every ending holds a sacred invitation not to despair, but to descend, to deepen, and to transform.

When I place a seed into the soil, I am practicing a quiet ritual of burial. I am not laying something to rest in grief, but planting it in faith. I do not expect it to remain the same. I know it must first break open in darkness. It must dissolve before it rises. This is the mystery of death and resurrection. Not a return to what was, but a surrender to what is becoming.

My work with plants is spiritual work. It is ancestral, feminine, and deeply intuitive. It has taught me to see the soil as a sacred womb, not a grave. Every time something falls away in my life, a relationship, a dream, or a version of myself, I remember the garden. I remember the leaves that fall without fear. I remember how the earth receives them without judgment, turns them into nourishment, and prepares them to bloom again in another form.

This is how I understand death now: not as disappointment, but as a process. A divine alchemical process that asks us to trust the unseen.

Being a plant mother has taught me that nothing truly dies, it transforms. It returns to the soil, to the womb, to spirit, to the source and it rises when the environment is right. Embracing Sacred Feminine cycles will energetically make our environment just right.

Beauty for ashes...

Sacred Feminine... Arise

Tools to Awaken your Inner Power

The Sacred Feminine is not a trend or a fleeting idea, it is an ancient, eternal force rising again. She's the soft power living deep within every woman and every soul who is seeking balance and to become whole through remembering the truth of your existence. Feminine energy is not demanding or hard, yet its power is felt through generations. Its presence is not forceful, yet it changes and replenishes everything it touches.

To awaken the Sacred Feminine is to return to the source and the cycles of creation.

It requires the death and burial of thoughts, habits and actions that block you from your highest self, the letting go of the past, the cleansing of memories that keep you bound and alchemizing those experiences that were painful and undesirable so that a new story and a new life can emerge.

You possess the resurrection power of transformation that always existed within you as a seed waiting to come forth and blossom with new fruit as a new creation.

You can reclaim your intuition, emotions, creativity, sensuality, and deep knowing, all qualities long suppressed in a world built on imbalance.

When we honor the Sacred Feminine, we do not discard the masculine; we restore the dance between both.

The Power of Letting Go

Rediscovering Feminine Power Through Detachment and Acceptance

When a woman chooses detachment, she is not giving up; she is letting go.

Letting go of control. Letting go of proving.

Letting go of the need to be affirmed.

Letting go of narratives that made her feel small, unworthy, or invisible.

Through detachment, the Sacred Feminine reclaims her energy. She unplugs from expectations, from roles that suffocate, from the noise of a world that profits from her exhaustion. In that holy release, she becomes sovereign. She no longer needs validation to feel valuable. She no longer begs love to stay. She no longer explains herself to be understood. She has practiced the art of not giving a f...

Detachment is her sacred boundary. It is the space where she can hear her intuition again. It is the moment she stops chasing and starts magnetically attracting. In this space, she doesn't just survive—she remembers her identity. She remembers that her power was never in holding on—it was always in her capacity to release with grace.

Through detachment, she transforms. She surrenders to her "soft power." She becomes unshakable and unbreakable, not because she is stoic and controlling, but because she no longer desires to control, or be owned by anything.

And in that freedom, she becomes autonomous and sacred.

Transformation Through Sacred Feminine Wisdom

Sacred Affirmation: "My vulnerability is my power, my intuition is my guide."

Sacred Feminine Practice: Begin each morning by placing your hand on your heart and speaking a blessing over yourself: "I bless this body, this heart, this soul. I walk today in grace and truth."

Sacred Reflection: In what ways have I been taught to dim my natural radiance, and how can I choose to shine now?

Sacred Prayer: Sacred Mother, Divine Source within me, I call back every piece of myself that I have given away in fear or forgotten in shame. I weave myself whole again with threads of love, courage, and ancient wisdom. Let me walk in the fullness of who I am meant to be. And so it is.

Part V:

Embrace The Reconnection & Restoration Through Sacred Feminine Wisdom

Chapter 7:

Feminine Archetypes and Sacred Practices to Support Balance and Transformation

Explore hidden truths, sacred rituals and habits that will deepen your understanding of femininity and womanhood, heal your wounds, help you to develop new mindsets and embody your divine nature, purpose and power to manifest a more abundant life and facilitate the transformation of a new society.

All these tools are necessary to fully embrace purpose, power, self-governance and become the image of God.

The Body: The Sacred Temple

Ayurveda, the "Science of Life," is more than a system of healing—it is a sacred path to wholeness. It teaches that we are not fragmented beings made of separate parts, but one complete organism, born of nature and woven from spirit, mind, and matter.

To live in health, we must live in harmony—with ourselves, our purpose, and the cycles of life.

At the heart of Ayurvedic philosophy is the understanding that body, mind, and spirit are reflections of the same energy. When one is disturbed, all are affected. When one is nurtured, all are elevated. Healing, then, is never isolated. It must touch all levels of our being.

In Ayurveda, the body is seen as a sacred vehicle—Deha, meaning "that which is burned," represents the body as both mortal and miraculous.

- We nourish the body with ahimsa (non-violence)—through food, touch, breath, and movement.
- The body is where we experience the world, and where spirit is housed.
- Keeping the body aligned with nature's rhythms (through diet, rest, and routine) anchors our energy and allows prana (life force) to flow.

The Mind: The Inner Instrument (Manas)

The mind is both messenger and maker. It shapes our perceptions, beliefs, and emotional tone. Ayurveda teaches that a clear, calm mind is essential for true health.

- Mental balance is cultivated through Sattva—purity, clarity, peace.
- Practices like meditation, mantra, journaling, and conscious breathing purify mental impressions (samskaras) and dissolve inner noise.
- When the mind is still, the soul is heard.

The Spirit (Atman): The Eternal Self

At the deepest level, Ayurveda teaches that we are not just bodies or thoughts—we are Atman, the timeless Self. Spirit is not something outside of us, but the very core of who we are.

- Connecting with spirit brings purpose, intuition, and deep inner peace.
- Through rituals, silence, sacred study, and devotion, we awaken the divine within.
- When body and mind are in harmony, the light of the spirit shines effortlessly.

The Path to Integration: Harmony Over Perfection

True health is not the absence of illness, it is the presence of balance. Ayurveda doesn't demand perfection. It invites awareness, alignment, and reverence.

When you eat with love, move with intention, think with clarity, and rest with grace you are living Ayurveda.

When you honor your cycles, trust your intuition, and speak to yourself gently, you are living Ayurveda.

When you see your body as sacred, your mind as a mirror, and your spirit as your compass you become whole.

This is the path of soft power.

Rooted. Intuitive. Sacred.

Becoming who you already are.

Always be a witness to your own being. Your mind, body and spirit are in constant communication. Your body uses the senses to signal wellness or disease. Your spirit sends downloads from the cosmos and all that is providing the seed of inner knowing. Your mind goes on a mission to seek out and follow up on the unctions that spirit has provided finding solutions, restoring wellness and welcoming ease.

"What heals in one season may harm in another."

- Adjust your diet, sleep, and lifestyle with the changing seasons.
- Cleanse or detox at seasonal junctions (especially spring and fall).
- Embrace seasonal rituals that support immune strength and inner balance.

You are the goddess becoming.

You are soft power.

You are Becoming Sacred.

Accept your power and purpose.

Acceptance: A Sacred Feminine Asset

Acceptance is the holy ground where healing begins.

In a world that teaches us to chase, fix, perfect, and prove acceptance is rebellion, but not a passive one. It is a sacred one.

Rooted in grace, guided by wisdom and held in the arms of the Divine Mother, acceptance is not to give up. It is to surrender control in service of truth.

It is to say: "I trust the timing. I trust the unfolding. I trust myself."

Sacred Feminine Knows

She knows how to hold what is, without rushing to change it.

She knows that pain must be witnessed to be transformed.

She understands that the seed must rest in the darkness before it ever dares to rise toward the light.

Acceptance is your superpower, because it embraces the strength of the present moment.

To Accept Is to Embody Soft Power

- It is embracing the body you're in, not just the one you're chasing.
- It is making peace with your past while still reaching for your future.

142

- It is knowing you are worthy, not once you're perfect, but right now.

The Sacred Feminine doesn't diminish or silence your desires. She simply reminds you that wholeness begins with allowing.

Ayurveda offers many practices that support healing and restoration of Sacred Feminine energy by bringing the body, mind, and spirit back into balance.

When I've not had a sacred practice, I've become unrooted, uncentered, and spiritually malnourished.

Without a sacred anchor, I've sometimes looked outside of myself for validation.

Life can sometimes pull us in every direction with trends, opinions, and expectations.
I have gone through seasons where I've struggled to make aligned decisions, because I've not grounded myself in inner truth. Sacred practices are what brings me back into my body in conscious awareness, as holy ground.

The life your body is living can often feel like an enemy or an afterthought and you live in your mind, anxious or scattered.

Without rituals or sacred intention, you may feel numb, cynical, or uninspired. Life becomes transactional rather than transformational. You find yourself just going through the motions.

Many people live out their lives in daily routines that feel unrewarding. I've actually talked to people that are resolved to this style of life. The only thing that feels good is shopping, sex, drugs or alcohol.

I've always known that there was something more for me to experience. I knew that my spirit guides and ancestors were with me. I connected with them in my spiritual practices, my rituals. I remember that I'm part of something ancient, eternal, and deeply intelligent.

An unrooted woman is easier to manipulate, monetize, or silence.

Without sacred rhythms (moon cycles, intention setting, rest rituals), time becomes a blur of doing, rather than being. You find yourself on a march toward burnout instead of a dance with life.

A sacred practice is a spiritual root system. It doesn't need to be elaborate, or super religious.

- It can be lighting a candle with intention
- Sitting in silence with your hand on your womb
- Walking barefoot and listening to the wind
- Journaling from your soul, not your mind

These small acts root you back into your essence, your divine codes, and your Sacred Feminine energy.

You become a goddess.

A goddess is more than just a mythological figure, she is an embodiment of divine feminine energy, a symbol of creation, intuition, sensuality, strength, and spiritual wisdom. She represents the sacred aspects of womanhood, nature, and cosmic balance and your soul remembers her well.

The Six Pillars of Feminine Healing

The six pillars of health provide a structured foundation for maintaining balance, resilience, and vitality in every area of life.

They are essential for the integration of Body, Mind, and Spirit. Each pillar addresses a key dimension of well-being. Together, they ensure no part of your "self" is neglected.

Balance and Prevention:

Pillars promote equilibrium (homeostasis), helping prevent disease before it starts, Ayurveda's core goal.

Daily Anchors:

They offer practical, repeatable habits (like sleep, diet, or meditation) that ground your day and reduce chaos.

Adaptability:

They serve as guiding principles you can adjust with life's seasons, stresses, and personal growth.

Self-Empowerment:

Understanding the pillars gives you the tools to take charge of your health physically, emotionally, and spiritually.

Think of them like the legs of a table: if one is weak or missing, the whole system becomes unstable.

Pillar # 1

Daily Routines and Self-Care

So while self-massage touches other pillars like movement, emotions, and even nutrition (via absorption), it most clearly belongs to Dinacharya, Ayurveda's way of honoring the body through sacred daily care.

Transformation Through Sacred Feminine Wisdom, Touch and Connection

Receiving and Giving Energy:

The hands are seen as extensions of the heart chakra, making them not only tools for physical action but also for giving and receiving love and energy.

In Ayurvedic massage (Abhyanga), the hands are used to apply herbal oils and stimulate marma points (vital energy points), similar to acupressure. The belief is that healing energy flows from the palms and fingertips.

Abhyanga (Self-Oil Massage)

Touch as Medicine:

Ayurveda teaches that touch is a form of spiritual communication. Self-massage is a way of returning to the body with reverence, acknowledging it as the vehicle of the soul (atman).

The origins of anointing with oil trace back thousands of years and appear across many ancient cultures each with unique but interconnected meanings. Here's a glimpse into its roots:

Ancient Egypt

- Priestesses and Priests used sacred oils in temple rituals to invoke gods and goddesses like Isis, Hathor, and Osiris.
- Anointing the head and body was believed to open spiritual gateways and preserve the soul's purity.
- Oils were infused with myrrh, frankincense, blue lotus, and other powerful plant allies.

Vedic India (Ayurveda)

- In Ayurveda, oils (sneha) were used not only for physical nourishment but as a spiritual balm, representing love.
- Abhyanga (oil massage) and anointing specific marma points were practices for healing, alignment, and spiritual clarity.
- The body was seen as a temple, and anointing honored the sacred self.

Ancient Israel and Mesopotamia

- Prophets, kings, and high priests were anointed with holy oils to mark their divine appointment or spiritual authority.
- The Hebrew word mashach means "to anoint"; from it comes Messiah ("anointed one").
- Oils were often mixed with herbs like cinnamon, cassia, and olive oil.

Christianity and Gnosticism

- Anointing became a symbol of spiritual awakening, healing, and divine favor.

- The "chrism" (consecrated oil) was used in baptisms, blessings, and mystical rites.
- Gnostic sects believed it was key to gnosis—inner divine knowledge.

Indigenous and Earth-Based Cultures

- Across African, Native American, and other indigenous traditions, plant-based oils, fats, and resins were used to connect with ancestors, spirits, and earth energy.
- Anointing was part of vision quests, rites of passage, and shamanic healing.

At its core, anointing is a bridge between human life and the divine, body and spirit, earth and the cosmos. It is an indigenous spiritual practice embraced by ancient cultures since the origin of humankind.

In the Bible, anointing was a deeply spiritual act, often done by others but sometimes performed by the individual themselves. It involved applying oil to the head or body, symbolizing healing, consecration, or joy. This practice aligns with the physical and energetic aspects of self-massage.

"But when you fast wash your face and anoint your head" (Matthew 6:17)

Here, Jesus encourages personal anointing during fasting—not for show, but as an inward posture of dignity and self-care. It reflects personal reverence and honoring the body as a temple.

Here is a massage to promote grounding and calmness:

Use warm sesame or almond oil, infused with rose, lavender, or shatavari.

Massage slowly in circular motions—especially around the breasts, womb, and feet—to reconnect with your body and calm the nervous system.

Do this before a warm bath or shower for grounding and nourishment.

The act of anointing with oil was intimate, embodied, and spiritually charged.

The powerful role of oil in anointing is both ancient and sacred. It symbolizes divine presence, healing, consecration, and transformation.

Across spiritual traditions and especially African, Biblical, Kemetic, and Indigenous practices, anointing with oil is not just a ritual; it's a transmission of power, intention, and blessing.

It echoes how self-massage when done with reverence can become a form of worship and sacred self-honoring.

Pillar #2

Meditation and Stress Management:

The Power of Breath

Healing through breath is one of the most ancient, powerful, and accessible practices for transforming the body, mind, and spirit. In many traditions, breath is life. Not just biologically, but energetically and spiritually. It's the bridge between the seen and unseen, between your physical body and your soul.

Breathing Activates the Parasympathetic Nervous System and Unlocks Rest

- Conscious, slow breathing shifts you out of fight-or-flight mode and into rest-and-digest.
- The vagus nerve is stimulated through breath, signaling the body it's safe to relax. Breathing slows and deepens, your heart rate naturally follows.
- This promotes deep physical rest, especially helpful for sleep, healing, or recovery from stress.

Connecting to Your Breath Slows the Heart Rate & Lowers Blood Pressure

- As breathing slows and deepens, your heart rate naturally follows.
- This promotes deep physical rest, especially helpful for sleep, healing, or recovery from stress.

Upon awakening in the morning, breathing is the first thing that enters my conscious awareness. During my sleep state my body is working, digesting, detoxing and regenerating. It is dreaming, traveling and experiencing life in other timelines. All of these activities, experiences and processes require energy. Morning meets me with a moment of replenishment. Breathing revitalizes me with energy, lowers my blood pressure, regulates my glucose and grounds me in conscious awareness. During the course of my day I take time to become aware of my breathing, reset and replenish.

The Breath Balances Energy Flow (Prana, Chi)

- In holistic and yogic traditions, breath is the carrier of life-force energy (prana).
- Steady breathing clears blockages in energy channels, bringing the body into harmony and homeostasis.

Increases Energy and Vitality

- Breath oxygenates the blood, nourishes cells, and boosts mental clarity and stamina.
- In pranayama (yogic breath control), specific techniques (like kapalabhati or nadi shodhana) clear energy channels, and awaken the inner fire (agni).

Aligns You Spiritually

- Breath is the sacred rhythm of the soul. When you breathe with awareness, you connect with the Divine within.
- In many traditions, breath is used to enter meditative and mystical states, opening the heart and crown chakras.

Here Is an Example of Coherent Breathing:

This is a simple and effective breathwork method that balances the nervous system and brings the body into a state of harmony.

How To:

- Inhale for 5 seconds
- Exhale for 5 seconds

- Repeat for at least 5 minutes
- Breathe in and out through the nose if possible
- Focus on smooth, even breaths
- Sit or lie down with a tall spine and relaxed body

Meditation

Origins of Meditation: A Global Inheritance

Meditation is one of the most ancient and powerful spiritual technologies known to humankind. Its origin spans cultures and continents, always rooted in the desire to connect with the Divine, access inner truth, and return to a state of oneness.

In a world that demands constant activity and endless distraction, meditation offers a sacred return, a way to reconnect with the self, to quiet the noise, and to access inner strength. Meditation is not merely a relaxation technique; it is a profound spiritual and physiological tool capable of transforming the mind, body, and spirit. Across cultures and centuries, meditation has been recognized for its power to heal, to reveal truth, and to restore balance.

At its core, meditation is the practice of intentional stillness. It invites the practitioner to observe their thoughts without judgment, to anchor their awareness in the present moment, and to access deeper layers of consciousness. Science increasingly confirms what ancient traditions have long taught: meditation changes the brain. Regular practice can shrink the amygdala, the part of the brain linked to fear and stress, while strengthening areas responsible for memory, empathy, and focus. These neurological shifts help explain why meditation reduces anxiety, improves emotional resilience, and sharpens mental clarity.

Physically, meditation has been shown to lower blood pressure, boost the immune system, reduce chronic pain, and even slow aging at the cellular level. By calming the nervous system, meditation allows the body to exit the chronic "fight or flight" mode and enter a state of rest, repair, and regeneration. The breath slows, the heart rate evens out, and energy begins to flow more freely throughout the body.

Yet the true power of meditation extends beyond measurable health benefits. Spiritually, meditation opens a portal to higher wisdom. In the stillness, one often encounters insights that elude the busy mind. One reconnects with their intuitive knowing, their inner sacredness, and, for many, a sense of oneness with all life. Meditation can dissolve the illusions of separation and scarcity, revealing the deeper truths of abundance, interconnectedness, and love.

Moreover, meditation empowers personal transformation. By witnessing one's own thought patterns without attachment, old stories of fear, shame, and limitation begin to unravel. New possibilities emerge. Over time, meditation can help break addictive cycles, heal emotional wounds, and guide the practitioner toward a life lived with greater authenticity, purpose, and peace.

Meditation is not a practice reserved for monks or mystics; it is accessible to all. Whether through silent sitting, mindful walking, prayerful reflection, or focused breathing, meditation adapts to the needs and culture of each practitioner. It requires no special tools or beliefs—only the willingness to be present.

The power of meditation lies in its simplicity and depth. It strengthens the mind, heals the body, and nourishes the spirit. In a world that often encourages disconnection, meditation calls us home to ourselves—to our breath, to our heartbeat, to the eternal space within. It is not an escape from life but a deeper engagement with it. In meditation, we do not abandon the world; we become more capable of living in it, fully awake and fully alive.

Meditation as a Vision Board

In meditation, the mind quiets enough to enter a state of expanded awareness. In this receptive state, it becomes possible to vividly see, feel, and experience desired realities as if they are already unfolding. Meditation removes the clutter of doubt and limitation, allowing the imagination to fully activate without resistance. In this space, your visions are not just mental concepts, they become living energies within your field, magnetizing the people, opportunities, and resources needed to bring them into form.

Unlike a traditional physical vision board, meditation makes your visions dynamic. You are not just observing them passively; you are stepping inside them. You can walk through the home you wish to live in, feel the joy of a healed relationship, embody the confidence of a thriving career, or experience the peace of a fully aligned life. By emotionally and energetically inhabiting your visions during meditation, you prime your subconscious mind to recognize and attract experiences that match the vibrational blueprint you have created.

Meditating as a vision board practice also enhances clarity. In stillness, you can discern which dreams are truly aligned with your soul, rather than the surface desires shaped by fear, comparison, or societal pressure. Often, new visions will emerge, ones you didn't even realize you were ready for because meditation connects you to the higher intelligence within.

Meditation amplifies trust. When you hold your visions internally, you are reminded that the real work of manifestation begins not outside, but within. You release the need to control every step, focusing instead on aligning your energy, your belief, and your actions with what you have already claimed in spirit.

I've experienced many life altering challenges in my lifetime. I know what it's like not having the tools to properly process undesired experiences such as hurt, loss, trauma and disease. I understand that these experiences magnetize on my energetic field providing contrast. What I truly desire, awaits my attraction to it and when I focus my heart, mind and spirit onto what I want rather than the thing I don't desire, I become energetically aligned and magnetized to it, attracting what I desire into my physical world.

Meditation and prayer allow me to usher my unwanted thoughts into the sea of forgetfulness. They are only as real as they are useful to support my ground state of conscious awareness, the empty canvas where my life's potential awaits my desire and creativity.

Meditation and prayer are two loaded weapons in my arsenal that I'll never return to their holsters.

Sitting in stillness and silence in meditation while listening to the voice of my creator and feeling the frequency of my collaboration with the universe, then articulating my awareness of its wholeness and abundance in prayer invites healing, acceptance, new insights and the space to receive and trust my instructions and "plan to goal."

How to Practice Meditation as a Vision Board:

- Begin with grounding breathwork to center your energy.
- Set a clear intention for what you want to create.
- Visualize your dream vividly: engage all the senses—see it, hear it, feel it, even smell and taste it.
- Allow emotions of gratitude, joy, and fulfillment to rise as if the vision is already real.
- Release the vision into the field with trust, knowing it is already unfolding.

Pillar #3

Movement – Engaging in regular physical activity that supports flexibility, strength, and mind-body connection (e.g., yoga, walking, dance).

In Ayurveda, movement is essential for maintaining the balance of your unique constitution called, (dosha) It stimulates digestive fire called (Agni), aiding in detoxification, and promoting mental clarity. It must always be approached with individuality and intention.

Tailored to Your Dosha:

Vata Types (light, mobile): Benefit from grounding, slow, and rhythmic movements like yoga, walking, or tai chi.

Pitta Types (intense, fiery): Need cooling, moderate-intensity activities like swimming, hiking in nature, or gentle martial arts.

Kapha Types (heavy, stable): Thrive with stimulating, dynamic workouts like brisk walking, cardio, or dance to overcome stagnation.

Daily Routine (Dinacharya): Ayurveda recommends regular movement—especially early in the morning—to align with natural rhythms, invigorate the senses, and aid elimination.

Detoxification (Ama Elimination): Physical activity helps remove toxins (ama) by increasing circulation, lymphatic flow, and sweat.

Mind-Body Connection: Movement is not just physical but also spiritual. Practices like yoga and pranayama are seen as moving meditation, enhancing prana (life force) and inner balance.

Balance, Not Burnout: Overexertion is discouraged. Movement should leave you energized, not depleted, in line with your current energy and season.

In Ayurveda, movement is sacred, intentional, and harmonizing, not just exercise for the sake of fitness.

Understanding and Identifying Your Fundamental Energy (Dosha)

A dosha is a fundamental energy or biological force that governs all physical and mental processes in the body and mind. There are three doshas, Vata, Pitta, and Kapha—and each one is made up of two of the five elements (space, air, fire, water, earth):

Vata Dosha (Air + Ether)

- Qualities: Light, dry, cold, mobile, irregular
- Governs: Movement, nerve impulses, breath, circulation, elimination
- Balanced Vata: Creativity, vitality, agility
- Imbalanced Vata: Anxiety, insomnia, dryness, constipation, overwhelm

Pitta Dosha (Fire + Water)

- Qualities: Hot, sharp, oily, intense, penetrating
- Governs: Digestion, metabolism, intellect, transformation
- Balanced Pitta: Focus, confidence, good digestion
- Imbalanced Pitta: Anger, inflammation, ulcers, perfectionism

Kapha Dosha (Earth + Water)

- Qualities: Heavy, slow, steady, smooth, cool, oily
- Governs: Structure, stability, immunity, lubrication
- Balanced Kapha: Calmness, strength, compassion
- Imbalanced Kapha: Lethargy, weight gain, congestion, attachment

Everyone has all three doshas, but in unique proportions, this is your prakriti (natural constitution). Imbalances or shifts in these energies (called vikriti) cause dis-ease or disharmony, and Ayurveda's goal is to restore balance through food, lifestyle, herbs, and mindfulness.

Pillar #4

Emotions – Cultivating emotional well-being by processing feelings, practicing forgiveness, gratitude, and fostering joy.

We've talked a lot about the power of emotions to sacred femininity and why patriarchy makes a concerted effort to suppress emotions. If you are unable to feel, you become unable to connect with your body, recognize imbalance or take authority of your own wellbeing.

In Ayurveda, emotions are deeply intertwined with physical health, and emotional balance is considered a core pillar of wellbeing. Emotions are not separate from the body, they influence digestion, immunity, energy flow, and even the balance of the doshas. Here's how Ayurveda views emotions as a pillar of health:

Mind-Body Connection (Manas & Sharira)

Ayurveda teaches that the mind (manas) and body (sharira) are inseparable. Unresolved emotions like anger, grief, fear, or jealousy can manifest as physical illness, just as physical imbalances can trigger emotional distress.

Doshas and Emotions

Each dosha is linked to specific emotional tendencies:

- Vata (Air + Ether): Tends toward fear, anxiety, worry when imbalanced.
- Pitta (Fire + Water): Experiences anger, frustration, irritability.
- Kapha (Earth + Water): Feels sadness, attachment, or depression when out of balance.

Balancing your dosha helps stabilize emotional responses.

Emotional Digestion (Mental Agni)

Just as we digest food, we must also "digest" experiences and emotions. Experiences just like food can impact your emotions as either, yum, or yuk. If we suppress or overindulge in emotional responses, it creates mental ama (toxic residue), leading to fatigue, confusion, or mental fog.

Sattva, Rajas, and Tamas (Gunas of the Mind)

Ayurveda describes three mental qualities:

- Sattva (clarity, peace, harmony) – Ideal state, cultivated through meditation, right living, pure diet.
- Rajas (activity, passion, restlessness) – Leads to anxiety, striving ambition, or anger when dominant.
- Tamas (inertia, darkness, ignorance) – Causes depression, lethargy, or denial.

In Ayurveda, emotional health means increasing Sattva, and reducing excessive Rajas and Tamas.

Healing Practices

To support emotional balance, Ayurveda recommends:

- Meditation & pranayama (breathwork)
- Mantra chanting
- Self-reflection or journaling
- Herbs like ashwagandha, brahmi, or tulsi
- A sattvic diet to calm the mind. "Sattva" means purity, harmony, and balance, and a Sattvic diet is designed to nourish not just the body, but also the mind and soul.

In essence, emotions in Ayurveda are treated with the same respect as physical symptoms. Emotional hygiene is health care, a crucial pillar for lasting harmony and vitality.

Faith and belief are necessary for any spiritual practice. Emotional balance is necessary to remove blockages in order to access and cultivate faith.

Proverbs 4:23 (NIV)

"Above all else, guard your heart, because everything you do flows from it."

The heart is the seat of emotional and spiritual life. When the heart is wounded or burdened, it can block faith. Guarding and healing your emotions is a way of protecting your spiritual flow.

The Bhagavad Gita 2:64-65

"But a disciplined person, who moves among sense objects, free from attachment and aversion, gains peace. In that peace, all pains are destroyed, and the intellect of such a person soon becomes steady."

Attachment and aversion are emotional disturbances that lead to suffering. When emotions are balanced, the mind becomes peaceful and receptive, making space for faith and intuitive wisdom.

Pillar #5

Nutrition

In the path of becoming sacred, how we nourish our bodies is a reflection of how we honor life itself. In Ayurveda, food is medicine, and the way we eat is as important as what we eat.

Every woman has a unique constitution, which governs her physical, emotional, and spiritual tendencies. When we eat in alignment with our constitution, we bring harmony to the body, mind, and energy field.

1.Eat with Awareness and Gratitude

- Meals are a form of prayer. Eating in silence or with presence transforms digestion.
- Say a blessing or take a few deep breaths before eating to invite sacred energy into your meal.

2. Choose Warm, Fresh, Cooked Foods

- Especially for women, warm and easily digestible foods nourish the womb and nervous system.
- Fresh, seasonal, local foods carry vital life force (prana).

3. Eat for Your Dosha

- Vata (air + ether): needs grounding, warming, oily foods like soups, stews, root vegetables, ghee.

- Pitta (fire + water): needs cooling, calming foods like sweet fruits, leafy greens, and coconut water.
- Kapha (earth + water): needs light, stimulating foods like steamed veggies, legumes, and spices.

4. Let Digestion Be Sacred

- No multitasking. No emotional eating.
- Eat only when hungry, stop when 75% full, and allow time between meals for proper digestion.

5. Use Spices as Medicine

- Spices like turmeric, cumin, fennel, ginger, and cardamom balance the doshas and awaken digestive fire (agni).
- Cooking with intention and healing herbs turns your kitchen into a sacred apothecary.

When a woman properly nourishes herself through Sacred Feminine practice, she doesn't just eat, she remembers. She honors her rhythms, her ancestral wisdom, and her sacred vessel.

Food becomes a ritual. Eating becomes prayer and the body becomes a temple of sacred power.

There's no such thing as "good" nutrition or "poor" nutrition. What you eat is either nutritious, or it isn't. Food that is absent of nutritional value is widely promoted in modern society, despite growing awareness of the importance of healthy eating. The promotion of foods that are void of nutritional value negatively impacts families.

One of the most pervasive ways that poor nutrition is promoted is through advertisements that target children.

Many ads for sugary cereals, fast food, candies, and snacks are shown during children's programming.

These foods are often high in sugar, salt, and unhealthy fats, contributing to poor dietary habits and long-term health issues like obesity, diabetes, and heart disease.

The use of cartoon characters, celebrities, and colorful packaging makes unhealthy foods appealing to children, making it harder for parents to resist these temptations.

Parents are unknowingly complicit, because these foods complement their "busy" lifestyles and they are being subliminally, socialized and programmed to accept the idea that if it's sold in a grocery store and if the FDA has approved it, it must not be that bad.

The health and wellbeing of families should be a high priority for us all.

I'm calling on women to arise and embrace their sacred power because Sacred Feminine is a healer and the kitchen is both the pharmacy and the core of the family's wellness.

The food industry profits most from processed, packaged, addictive foods—loaded with sugar, salt, and chemicals designed to trigger cravings, not satiation. These foods are cheaper to produce, easier to market, and far more profitable than whole, fresh, nutrient-dense foods. The result? A society addicted to food that leaves the body malnourished, inflamed, and depleted—especially in marginalized communities.

Food targeting women are marketed as "low-fat," "guilt-free," and "skinny" foods under the guise of wellness, but these are often stripped of any real nutrients and full of preservatives.

Mothers are sold convenient, processed snacks for kids that are flashy but lack fiber, vitamins, or real ingredients.

The emotional hook? "You're a good mom if you buy this. You're a sexy woman if you eat this."

Fast food and soda companies spend billions advertising, especially in low-income and food desert communities, where fresh food may be scarce. Meanwhile, nutrition education is minimal, and access to clean, organic, or culturally-relevant foods is often limited to wealthier zip codes.

Ancestral and Indigenous food systems once rooted in healing, balance, and connection to the land are often dismissed, demonized, or "gentrified."

Food isn't just fuel—it's vibrational energy, medicine, and a reflection of how we care for ourselves in a world that often asks us to give more than we receive.

Pillar #6

Sleep

Sleep is one of the core foundations of overall health, just as essential as nutrition, movement, and mental wellbeing. It's during sleep that the body and mind undergo critical restorative processes.

Sleep provides both physical restoration and cellular repair.

- During deep sleep, your body repairs tissues, muscles, and organs.
- Quality sleep strengthens the immune system, helping the body fight infections and recover faster.
- Sleep regulates hormones, including those for stress (cortisol), appetite (ghrelin and leptin), and growth.
- Sleep helps store and organize memories, improving learning and decision-making.

- Adequate rest enhances focus, creativity, and problem-solving.
- Poor sleep increases the risk of anxiety, depression, and irritability.
- Lack of sleep can increase hunger and cravings, especially for sugary or fatty foods.
- Sleep supports cardiovascular function and helps regulate blood pressure.
- Sleep impacts how the body processes insulin, affecting diabetes risk.

Well rested individuals cope better with stress and emotional challenges.

Sleep, especially deep and dream state sleep can be a space for intuitive messages and inner reflection.

Making sleep a priority can transform your health. Prioritize 7–9 hours of quality sleep per night, create a calming nighttime routine, and honor rest as a sacred act of self-care.

I find it interesting that rest and quality sleep is associated with laziness. I've discovered that when women are physically and emotionally out of balance, they are always stating how tired they feel, but at the same time seem to defend the reasons for their fatigue.

Patriarchy doesn't value sleep or rest. It prefers to have the masses of human beings working as wealth generating resources for its few beneficiaries, 24 hours a day, 7 days a week. You can sleep when you're dead, is their mantra.

Transformation Through Sacred Feminine Wisdom

Sacred Affirmation: "I reclaim my voice, my space, my body and my sacred rhythm. My intuition is my guide, and I trust her fully. My hands are tools for sacred touch and healing."

Feminine Archetypes are Powerful Mirrors for Reconnecting with the Feminine Energy

We dress for the impact that our outer appearance might have on who we are and what we want to communicate about ourselves, outwardly.

The history of using clothing to express identity is rich, rooted in culture, spirituality, class, and personal transformation.

Throughout history, clothing and makeup have never been merely decorative.

They are sacred signals—rituals of identity, tools of power, and mirrors of a society's values and hierarchies.

Especially for women and feminine embracing beings, adornment has been both a symbol of subjugation and a source of sacred power.

When we dress ourselves, we are often stepping into an archetype. Feminine archetypes such as sage, queen, maiden, mother, warrior—have long been shaped by the visible and invisible lines of caste, class, and colonial systems.

Feminine archetypes serve a similar purpose to wardrobe: they are expressions of identity, intention, and energetic embodiment. Just as we choose clothes to reflect who we are becoming, we also consciously or unconsciously embody archetypes to shape how we live, love, and lead.

The Sacred Feminine lives within every woman, waiting to be remembered. She shows up in many forms, wearing many faces, each one an archetype, each one a key. By understanding and embodying these feminine archetypes, you can begin to unlock parts of yourself that have been hidden, shamed, or forgotten.

These archetypes are more than symbols—they are living energies, sacred guides on the path to wholeness. They don't demand perfection. They simply invite presence. They make space for you to experience yourself as a new energetic being.

You can experience these sacred, transformative archetypes through affirmations, fashion and adornment, colors, scents and however you become inspired to embrace them.

The Maiden Archetype

Essence:

The Maiden embodies youth, curiosity, new beginnings, and untamed potential. She is the spark of possibility, the dreamer, the explorer, the innocent soul unburdened by the world's expectations. Her power lies in her openness, joy, and willingness to say yes to life.

Core Qualities:

Innocence: Sees the world with fresh eyes, unjaded and full of wonder.

Curiosity: Asks questions, follows her intuition, seeks new experiences.

Playfulness: Embraces joy, movement, spontaneity, and fun.

Rebirth: Symbolizes the beginning of cycles, springtime energy, and self-discovery.

Purity of Purpose: Acts from an authentic, soul-aligned place—not performance, but presence.

Sacred Affirmation:

"I welcome the beauty of new beginnings and trust the unfolding of my journey."

Guided Prompts:

Inner Innocence: What did you love as a child that still brings you joy today?

Fresh Start: What area of your life is calling for a fresh, unburdened approach?

Curious Heart: Where can you give yourself permission to explore without a goal or outcome?

Maiden Boundaries: Where might naivety or people-pleasing need stronger self-trust and clarity?

Spring Within: What is trying to bloom inside you right now?

Ritual to Invoke the Maiden

Play Day: Plan a day (or hour) with no agenda—follow joy. Dance, paint, walk barefoot, sing out loud. Let your inner girl lead.

Flower Offering: Pick or buy fresh flowers, symbolizing your inner bloom. Place them on your altar and thank your Maiden self for her courage to begin.

Innocence Letter: Write a letter to your younger self—from love, not correction. Acknowledge her magic, her bravery, and her wild wonder.

Visual & Design Ideas:

Color Palette: Soft pastels—lavender, blush, peach, pale gold.

Symbols: Spring flowers, butterflies, crescent moon, dawn light, flowing dresses.

Imagery: A barefoot girl in a meadow, gazing at the stars, or holding a lantern in the dark.

The Maiden teaches us that it is sacred to begin again—to live in wonder, to chase beauty, and to trust the path even when it's unwritten. She is not weak, she is brave in her vulnerability and radiant in her becoming.

After departing a decades-long marriage during my sixtieth return around the sun, I have invoked the maiden in order to rebrand and revitalize my life. Embracing the Maiden helped me see myself not as someone who "lost" a relationship, but as someone who gained herself. I have stepped into a vibrational rebirth where I have redefined my beauty, ambition, love, and joy on my own sacred terms. I no longer wait to be chosen, I have chosen myself. I remember a younger, hopeful, more inspired version of myself. I am dreaming again and the possibilities of my life are seemingly endless.

Celebrities who embody the Maiden archetype through their style, public energy, career choices, or emotional openness. These women radiate qualities like innocence, newness, sensitivity, creativity, and romantic expression, often paired with growth into deeper archetypes over time:

Tracee Ellis Ross

- Why: Tracee radiates a playful, curious, and joyfully expressive spirit. She often dances, plays with fashion, and shares openly about her inner world.
- Maiden Traits: Light-hearted, whimsical, emotionally expressive, in love with life.

Marsai Martin

- Why: Marsai carries an innocent confidence—balancing sweetness, ambition, and joy as a rising creative force.
- Maiden Traits: Bright-eyed, playful, emerging creative power with a youthful lens.

Olivia Rodrigo

- Why: Her music, especially the SOUR era, embodies the emotional waves, longing, and self-discovery of the Maiden.
- Maiden Traits: Vulnerability, heartbreak, identity-seeking, and youthful rebellion.

The Mother Archetype

Essence:

The Mother is the archetype of unconditional love, nurturing, creation, and sacred responsibility. She gives life—not only biologically, but through ideas, communities, art, and healing. Her power is rooted in her ability to hold, nourish, and grow everything she touches.

Core Qualities:

Nurturance: Offers deep care, compassion, and emotional nourishment.

Creation: Brings life into form—whether through birth, projects, or transformation.

Protection: Safeguards what is sacred with fierce, grounded strength.

Devotion: Lives in service to growth without losing herself in sacrifice.

Emotional Depth: Holds space for grief, joy, fear, and hope with an open heart.

Being a mother causes a woman to be laid bare in many ways. Childbirth itself is the beginning of her selflessness. The depth of my emotional experiences as a mother has extended from joy to unimaginable grief. In my life I've experienced the expectation and excitement of birth and the dread, disappointment and finality of the death of both a child and marriage. Deep nurturing, self-care and self-compassion has healed and sustained me on a daily basis.

Sacred Affirmation:

"I am a vessel of love, a nurturer of life, and a guardian of sacred growth."

Guided Prompts:

Womb Wisdom: What are you currently nurturing—emotionally, spiritually, or creatively?

Balanced Care: Where are you giving too much without receiving? Where do you need to replenish?

Creation Energy: What wants to be born through you right now?

Sacred Protection: What or whom are you called to protect with fierce love?

Mothering Yourself: How can you offer yourself the tenderness you give to others?

Ritual to Invoke the Mother

Sacred Offering: Create an altar with items that represent birth, abundance, and care—fruit, milk, flowers, womb imagery, or ancestral tokens.

Nourishment Practice: Prepare a meal or drink with full intention, blessing each ingredient. As you eat or drink, honor the sacred act of receiving care.

Womb Meditation: Place hands on your womb (physical or energetic) and breathe deeply. Visualize golden light radiating from it, sending healing, creation, and peace into the world.

Visual & Design Ideas:

Color Palette: Earth tones, soft reds, terracotta, ivory, deep greens.

Symbols: Full moon, tree, nest, womb, milk, cradle, earth.

Imagery: A woman holding the earth in her hands, pregnant with light, or wrapped in a shawl with stars woven into it.

Michelle Obama

- Why: She radiates protective, wise, and nurturing energy—not just to her daughters, but to an entire generation. Through her advocacy, warmth, and steadiness, she is a collective mother figure.
- Mother Traits: Strength, grace, leadership, emotional intelligence, nourishment.

Oprah Winfrey

- Why: Oprah has served as a spiritual and emotional nurturer for millions through storytelling, listening, and guiding others to self-heal.
- Mother Traits: Wisdom, mentorship, holding space, generational healing.

I also embody the Mother archetype. I'm always in a perpetual state of teaching, healing, and nurturing. The mother archetype generates my, "why" and it is at the core of my service and reason for being.

The Huntress Archetype

Essence:

The Huntress is the fierce, independent, and untamed force of the Sacred Feminine. She is the archetype of focus, self-sovereignty, wild instinct, and freedom. Rooted in nature, purpose, and clarity of vision, she protects her boundaries, pursues her goals, and lives on her own terms.

Core Qualities:

Independence: Free-spirited, self-reliant, and unconcerned with external approval.

Focus: Knows what she wants and takes direct, aligned action toward it.

Wildness: Embraces instinct, nature, and untamed feminine power.

Sisterhood: Protects and uplifts other women; she honors the tribe but needs solitude.

Sacred Purpose: Follows her inner compass and lives with mission and meaning.

After times of heartbreak, loss, or deep transition, the Huntress energy helped me remember that I am whole within myself. She whispered to me: "You do not have to wait for anyone to rescue you."

When I made choices purely for my growth, starting a new project, traveling alone, setting new boundaries, I was embodying the Huntress, trusting my own instincts rather than seeking external approval.

Sacred Affirmation:

"I walk my path with clarity, courage, and unwavering devotion to my soul's purpose."

Guided Prompts

Sacred Target: What are you aiming for right now? What's calling your full presence and precision?

Wild Freedom: Where in your life do you crave more freedom, solitude, or wild expression?

Instinct & Intuition: How often do you trust your gut? What does your inner wild woman say?

Boundary Check: Where do you need to reclaim space, time, or energy to stay aligned?

Purpose Activation: What purpose feels so true that you'd follow it through the forest?

Ritual to Invoke the Huntress

Nature Walk (Silent Tracking): Walk alone in nature. Move in silence. Listen to the wind, your breath, your steps. Ask the land to show you where you are being called.

Arrow Meditation: Close your eyes. Visualize holding a bow and arrow. Set your intention as the arrow. Breathe deeply, aim, and "release" it into the universe.

Claiming Space: Stand with your feet wide, arms open. Speak aloud your truth—what you stand for, what you will no longer tolerate, and what you are pursuing. Let your voice echo with power.

Visual & Design Ideas:

Color Palette: Forest green, charcoal, deep browns, silver moonlight.

Symbols: Bow and arrow, moon, wolf, deer, wildflowers, trees.

Imagery: A woman standing in a forest, moonlight on her skin, bow in hand, eyes locked on the unseen horizon.

The Huntress reminds us that being feminine doesn't necessarily mean being soft or passive. She has fierce devotion, sharp instinct, and wild grace. When you walk in her energy, you say yes to freedom, purpose, and the power of a woman who knows exactly who she is.

Serena Williams

- Why: Serena's athletic dominance, unshakable determination, and resilience under pressure define the Huntress. She channels strength, discipline, and a sacred warrior spirit.
- Huntress Traits: Physical power, purpose-driven, boundary-setter, goal-oriented.

Angela Bassett

- Why: Angela often plays powerful, no-nonsense women who lead with conviction and presence. In real life, she exudes strength, grace, and unapologetic self-worth.
- Huntress Traits: Commanding, loyal, strategic, emotionally powerful.

The Sage Archetype

Essence:

The Sage is the embodiment of deep wisdom, clarity, and truth. She is the teacher, the truth-teller, the guide who illuminates the path not by emotion or impulse—but by insight, experience, and discernment. Her power lies in her stillness, intellect, and devotion to higher knowledge.

Core Qualities:

Wisdom: Draws from life experience, inner knowing, and ancient truths.

Discernment: Sees beyond illusion; knows when to speak and when to stay silent.

Clarity: Offers guidance that is rooted in truth, not ego or emotion.

Detachment: Witnesses rather than react; holds space without judgment.

Mentorship: Shares her knowledge not to control, but to empower.

Sacred Affirmation:

"I am the voice of timeless wisdom. I see clearly, I speak truth, and I lead with soul."

Guided Prompts

Inner Council: What is your inner wise woman whispering to you right now?

Life Lessons: What truths have your lived experiences taught you that no book could?

Sacred Silence: When was the last time you allowed silence to speak louder than your words?

Teaching with Grace: Where in your life can you guide others without needing to be "right"?

Truth Alignment: Are your words and choices in alignment with what you deeply know?

Ritual to Invoke the Sage

Wisdom Meditation: Sit quietly with a journal and candle. Ask your higher self: What do I know that I've forgotten? Let the answers flow without judgment.

Symbol of Truth: Choose an object (crystal, feather, scroll) to represent your Sage self. Hold it during moments when you need clarity or guidance.

Sacred Reading Practice: Select a passage from a sacred text or meaningful book. Reflect on it as a spiritual teaching, then write your personal interpretation.

Visual & Design Ideas:

Color Palette: Deep indigo, smoky gray, ivory, dark gold.

Symbols: Owl, ancient book, staff, lantern, scrolls, tree of life.

Imagery: A woman seated under a full moon, writing by candlelight, cloaked in silence and depth.

Embodying the Sage invites you to trust your lived truth, to find power in stillness, and to teach from a place of deep self-knowledge. She reminds us that wisdom is not loud—it is rooted, sacred, and eternal.

The Sage helps me reflect on past experiences, not as burdens, but as stepping stones to deeper self-awareness. Through this reflection, I learned to integrate the lessons from past mistakes and triumphs, using them to guide my current decisions and shape my future with greater wisdom.

In the process of healing from past emotional wounds or mistakes, the Sage inspired me to look back at the situations with compassion and objectivity. I saw how each experience, no matter how difficult, has contributed to my growth. This shift in perspective has allowed me to let go of regret and embrace the full richness of my life's journey.

Examples of the Sage:

Maya Angelou

- Why: Maya was a quintessential Sage—sharing profound truths about love, trauma, resilience, and womanhood through poetry and presence.
- Sage Traits: Storykeeper, wise teacher, soul speaker, spiritual authority.

Yara Shahidi

- Why: Yara is deeply thoughtful, politically conscious, and carries herself with grace and intellectual poise far beyond her years.
- Sage Traits: Articulate, wise, values justice, self-aware, thoughtful communicator.

The Lover Archetype

Essence:

The Lover embodies sensuality, magnetism, connection, and the sacred art of presence. She lives through the body, heart, and senses—awakening joy, intimacy, and creativity wherever she goes.

Core Qualities

Embodiment: Fully inhabits her body with pleasure, awareness, and reverence.

Magnetism: Attracts through authenticity and radiant self-love.

Connection: Values intimacy with self, others, and the divine.

Creativity: Channels emotion and desire into art, beauty, and expression.

Pleasure as Power: Honors desire and joy as sacred gateways to the divine.

Sacred Affirmation:

"I honor my body as a temple of pleasure, power, and divine connection."

Guided Prompts

Body Love: What is one way you can honor or celebrate your body today?

Desire Check-In: What do you truly desire—not just sexually, but emotionally and spiritually?

Pleasure Rituals: How can you create more beauty, softness, or sensuality in your daily routine?

Self-Intimacy: What makes you feel deeply seen, heard, or touched? Can you offer that to yourself now?

Sacred Connection: How does your sensuality connect you to something greater—nature, spirit, or soul?

Visual & Design Ideas:

Color Palette: Rose, blush pinks, soft reds, gold, warm amber.

Symbols: Roses, doves, hearts, silk, fire, perfume bottles, flowing water.

Imagery: A woman bathing in moonlight, lying in a field of roses, or dancing in soft fabric under the sun.

Embracing the Lover archetype is about more than romance—it's about becoming your own beloved. She reminds us that joy, connection, and desire are sacred—and that to love deeply is to live fully.

The Lover archetype is the heartbeat of feminine transformation. She is the part of me that feels deeply, opens fully, and connects passionately with life, beauty, and spirit. While the Sage offers wisdom and clarity, the Lover brings vitality, emotion, sensuality, and soulful connection. She reminds me that to be fully alive is to be fully engaged with my senses, my heart, my creativity, and my sacred desires.

The Lover reminds me that I am inherently worthy not because of what I achieve or how others see me, but simply because I exist. She teaches me that love must first be cultivated within, and that true self-love is the foundation for every healthy relationship, dream, and creative endeavor.

Rihanna

- Why: Rihanna embodies unapologetic sensual power and sexual confidence while also showing emotional realness. She balances softness with fierce allure.
- Lover Traits: Bold sensuality, self-love, aesthetic mastery, fearless intimacy.

Toni Braxton

- Why: Toni's voice, presence, and style have always been deeply sensual. Even now, she moves with the confident grace of a woman who owns her softness and power.
- Lover Traits: Mature sensuality, emotional transparency, seductive poise.

THE QUEEN ARCHETYPE

Essence:

She is sovereign, centered, and devoted—to herself, her purpose, and her people. The Queen governs with both strength and grace. She knows her worth and sets the tone for how she is treated. She leads with her presence, not just her words.

Core Traits:

- Dignified
- Self-respecting
- Supportive leader
- Strategic and wise
- Grounded in purpose
- Powerful yet nurturing
- Legacy-minded

Queen Energy Looks Like:

- Knowing when to say yes with grace and no with authority
- Making decisions from vision, not validation
- Holding space for others to shine—without dimming your own light
- Walking into a room and changing the atmosphere just by being there
- Practicing discernment, not just power
- Expecting respect, loyalty, and devotion—and giving the same
- Resting in your worth, not chasing worthiness

Queen Affirmations

- "I am the ruler of my own energy."
- "I am not afraid to be seen in my power."
- "My boundaries are loving and firm."
- "I serve without shrinking."
- "I lead with vision, grace, and devotion."

Beyoncé (as Queen-Mother blend)

- Why: Beyoncé has become the cultural embodiment of the Queen—curating her image, empire, and impact with intention and deep devotion to legacy.
- Queen Traits: Sovereignty, creative direction, ancestral leadership, divine feminine embodiment.

Queen Latifah

- Why: A literal and symbolic Queen, she has led with versatility and grace across music, acting, and cultural impact—always with self-respect.
- Queen Traits: Legacy builder, loyalty, grounded confidence, command.

Normani

- Why: She moves with quiet confidence, intention, and mystery. Her silence speaks power.
- Queen Traits: Magnetism, strength, autonomy, quiet command.

It's important for goddess energy to be acknowledged. Feminine archetypes grant an invitation for them to join in your transformation.

The goddess moves through you in many forms: soft, wild, wise, sensual, fierce, nurturing, and sovereign. These forms are not outside of you. They are archetypes living in your soul's memory. When you honor them, you awaken divine aspects of your own being.

Part VI:
Maintain The Balance

Chapter 8:

Understanding the Masculine and Feminine Dance and the Daily Sacred Practices That Help Maintain Balance

We need the balance of masculine and feminine energy in order to thrive and evolve as individuals, women and as a species. We simply cannot continue to prefer one vibration over another.

We live in a world that has long tilted toward the masculine, not the Sacred Masculine, but a distorted one: all doing, striving, building, conquering. In that tilt, we've been taught that power is hard, progress is fast, and stillness is weakness.The truth is this: power without softness is brittle. Movement without meaning lacks purpose, and masculinity without the presence of the feminine creates imbalance.

Masculine–feminine integration is the inner process of balancing two core energies—the masculine (yang) and the feminine (yin)—that exist within every person, regardless of gender. This balance leads to wholeness, emotional harmony, purpose, and power.

A deeper understanding of masculine and feminine characteristics:

Feminine Energy

- Being

- Intuition
- Flow
- Receptivity
- Emotion
- Creation
- Connection
- Inner world
- Softness, surrender, nurturing

Masculine Energy

- Doing
- Logic
- Structure
- Direction
- Discipline
- Protection
- Provision
- Outer world
- Strength, clarity, focus

The truth is that the masculine and feminine are not in opposition; they are in divine partnership. They are not about gender, but about energy. They live in all of us, and they long to dance in harmony.

When these energies are integrated rather than competing, a person becomes:

- Grounded and intuitive
- Assertive yet compassionate
- Able to receive and create, but also plan and act
- Emotionally intelligent and purpose-driven
- Soft and strong, inwardly connected and outwardly clear

Examples of Integration

- A woman who confidently leads a business (masculine) while staying attuned to her emotional cycles and intuitive wisdom (feminine).
- A man who protects and provides (masculine) but can openly express his feelings and hold emotional space (feminine).
- Creative flow (feminine) channeled into an organized structure like a book, making a business, or a community project out of it (masculine).

The masculine holds structure, direction, and clarity. It is the mountain, the container, the sacred protector. The feminine is flow, intuition, and creation. She is the river, the mystery, the fertile ground where life is conceived. The masculine penetrates; the feminine receives. The masculine acts; the feminine feels. But both are needed for true wholeness.

When the Sacred Feminine is absent, we forget how to listen. We lose connection to the womb of wisdom, our bodies, our emotions, and our intuition. When the Sacred Masculine is absent, we lose our sense of grounded purpose. We become anxious and overfeeling, and unprotected.

But when they are united, there is a sacred balance: the masculine creates the path, and the feminine chooses the direction; the masculine provides the foundation, and the feminine fills it with life.

This is the truth of balance: we need both. We are both. And healing happens when we allow them to meet not in war, but in love.

The feminine without the masculine may feel deeply, but not move. The masculine without the feminine may move, but forget why. Together, they serve a sacred purpose. Sacred power and presence.

Balance is not 50/50. It is the right relationship. It is listening to what is needed now, and honoring it fully. It is letting the feminine lead from the heart and the masculine follow through with devotion to purpose and mission at hand.

As a woman walking the path of Sacred Feminine embodiment, I have had to heal both energies within me. I've had to learn that softness is not weakness, that stillness is not laziness, that rest is not resistance—it is restoration. I've also had to reclaim the Sacred Masculine, not the one that rushes, pushes, and forces, but the one that holds, supports, and honors. The part of me that takes action in service of my truth.

This is not just healing for individuals, but it is healing for the planet.

Because when the Sacred Feminine rises, and the Sacred Masculine remembers her, we return to wholeness.

We return to our ground state. We return to the truth. We return to love.

Sacred Affirmation:

"I accept myself as I am.

I honor the season I'm in.

I release the war within.

And I return to love."

Chapter 9:

Returning to Sacred Feminine Balance and Power

The Rise, Fall, and Future of Matriarchal Societies

Throughout human history, there have been societies where the Sacred Feminine was not just honored, it was central.

These cultures, often matriarchal or matrilineal in structure, flourished in ways that fostered harmony, sustainability, and communal wellbeing.

They thrived not through dominance, but through deep connection with the Earth, the cycles of life, and the divine wisdom of the feminine principle.

Sacred Feminine energy is not about gender, it is an archetypal force. It is receptive, nurturing, intuitive, creative, and regenerative. It governs the moon, the waters, the womb, and the mysteries of life and death. It is also powerful, not in the way of conquest, but in the way of deep knowing, healing, and embodiment.

When honored in society, this energy gives rise to leadership that listens more than it speaks, heals more than it harms, and builds more than it breaks.

Matriarchal Societies of Africa: The Roots of Sacred Feminine Power

Long before colonial maps and patriarchal structures reshaped the Alkebulan (the motherland) into the continent of Africa, there were societies where women held sacred power—not just within the home, but in the spiritual, political, and economic life of the people. In these matriarchal or matrilineal societies, the Sacred Feminine was not symbolic—it was embodied in leadership, law, lineage, and land.

Alkebulan, aka Africa is the cradle of humanity, it also holds the deepest roots of Sacred Feminine wisdom. From priestess-queens and matrilineal clans to goddess-based cosmologies, many African societies once flourished by honoring the divine balance of masculine and feminine energy.

Key Examples of Matriarchal or Matrilineal African Societies

The Akan (Ghana and Ivory Coast)

The Akan people follow a matrilineal inheritance system, where lineage and succession pass through the mother's bloodline.

Women, especially the queen mothers (Ohemaa), wield great influence in political affairs. They advise kings, select future chiefs, and are often seen as spiritual guardians of the land. The Ohemaa embodies the Sacred Feminine as a leader, healer, and intercessor with the ancestors.

In the heart of West Africa, particularly in Ghana and parts of Côte d'Ivoire, the Akan people have for centuries maintained a matrilineal social system that serves as a profound example of sacred balance between masculine and feminine energies. Their culture offers a living blueprint for how societies can thrive when leadership, lineage, and law are structured not through domination or binary hierarchies—but through interdependence, spiritual reverence, and ancestral wisdom.

The Igbo (Nigeria)

Although the Igbo are often described as patriarchal today, traditionally they had dual-sex political systems, where women had their own assemblies, courts, and market governance.

Titles such as Omu or female chiefs held sacred authority.

The goddess Ala, the Earth Mother, was central to Igbo cosmology, overseeing morality, fertility, and ancestral connection.

The Tuareg (Sahara Desert region – Mali, Niger, Algeria)

These Berber-speaking, semi-nomadic people maintain a matrilineal system. They owned tents, livestock, and inheritance rights.

Tuareg women are also the primary custodians of the written script (Tifinagh) and oral traditions, reinforcing their cultural and spiritual authority.

The Lovedu (South Africa)

The Lovedu people are centered around a Rain Queen, a sacred female ruler believed to control rainfall and fertility of the land.

The Rain Queen is not a figurehead, she is revered as a living goddess, mediating between the people, ancestors, and the natural world.

Her leadership reflects a Sacred Feminine principle: nurturing the earth, ensuring abundance, and keeping balance.

The Dahomey (present-day Benin)

While the Dahomey Kingdom had kings, women played dominant military and spiritual roles.

The famous Dahomey Amazons—an elite all-female warrior group—protected the kingdom and embodied both fierce feminine strength and sacred service.

Female deities, ancestral queens, and priestesses held high status in religious life.

In these societies, the Sacred Feminine was not just political, it was cosmic. Women were not "equal" in a Western feminist sense; rather, they were sacred conduits of life, continuity, and divine will.

The Earth was Mother. Fertility was power. Elders and ancestors moved through the matriline. Leadership wasn't about dominance, it was about custodianship and connection.

These societies understood something the modern world has nearly forgotten: that to honor the feminine is to remain in balance with the Earth, the body, and the soul of a people.

Colonialism, and patriarchal religions (including Christianity and Islam in certain forms), and the globalization of Western gender norms eroded many of these traditions and shifted society. Women's power was diminished, Sacred Feminine practices were demonized, and male-dominated structures were imposed.

Yet traces remain,especially in the reverence for mothers, the resilience of market women, and the wisdom keepers of ancestral traditions.

Matriarchal societies that flourished in early human societies often operated under the guidance of the feminine principle.

Cultures like those of Çatalhöyük in Anatolia, the Minoans of Crete, and the Iroquois Confederacy in North America revered the Earth as Mother and held the roles of women—and the energy of feminine wisdom—in the highest regard.

These societies were characterized by:

- Shared leadership and consensus decision-making.
- Worship of goddesses and the Earth as divine.
- Matrilineal lineage, where inheritance and identity came through the mother's line.
- Communal child-rearing, food sharing, and cooperation over competition.

In many Indigenous and ancestral societies—especially across Africa, the Caribbean, and parts of Asia and the Americas—children were never raised by parents alone. Instead, they were nurtured by the village, the clan, the extended family. This practice, known as communal child-rearing, was not merely practical—it was sacred.

At its heart, communal parenting is a living expression of balance—a weaving together of feminine and masculine energies, of individual and collective wisdom, of personal care and social responsibility. In honoring the sacred balance between roles, generations, and energies, communal child-rearing creates a world in which everyone belongs, everyone contributes, and no child is left unseen. I grew up in a community that reflected many of these characteristics. It made me feel a great sense of belonging and created an extension of my own family.

In many ancient societies, especially those grounded in matriarchal or balance-based worldviews, governance was not built on domination, but on harmony.

- Leadership was sacred.
- Decision-making was communal.
- Power was not wielded to conquer others but to maintain balance within the people and with the Earth.
- Peace-oriented governance offered fewer signs of warfare or conquest.

These were not societies where women dominated men, but rather where feminine values guided collective life. Masculine and feminine energy coexisted in balance, not in opposition.

Why They Fell

Over time, these matriarchal or balanced societies were often overtaken by patriarchal systems rooted in hierarchy, control, a caste system of organization in which individuals or groups are ranked one above the other based on status, authority, or power.

It is a top-down structure where decisions, commands, and control flow from those at the top to those at the bottom.

The hierarchical need for expansion may appear complex, but it arises from the way power is structured and maintained in top-down systems. Hierarchies, especially those rooted in domination (rather than service or balance), often require constant growth, control, or acquisition to sustain their authority.

This leads to cycles of conquest, colonization, and exploitation—not because expansion is necessary for survival, but because it reinforces the hierarchy itself.

In every corner of the modern world, patriarchy exerts a tightening grip—not always through violence or law, but often through tradition, religion, and inherited power structures. Though it masquerades as order, protection, or even progress, patriarchal dominance has become one of the greatest obstacles to humanity's evolution. It blocks our ability to grow into wholeness by denying half of our sacred design: The Sacred Feminine.

Project 2025—is backing a patriarchal and monotheistic agenda aimed at enforcing traditional gender roles: limiting access to historical truth in education, undermining equality across every sector of society and suppressing Sacred Feminine energy.

The rise of monotheism gradually replaced goddess worship with male gods and male authority.

The idea of monotheism emerged during a time when rising empires sought to consolidate power not only over land and people, but over faith itself. Faith is the substance of things hoped for and the evidence of things not yet seen.

By centering divinity into a singular, masculine form—often depicted as a distant, authoritative father figure—monotheism disrupts the ancient, cyclical, earth-based spiritual systems that honored both feminine and masculine forces in balance. Where once goddesses were revered as life-givers, healers, and protectors of nature, they were now erased, demonized, or made subordinate. This shift interrupted humanity's relationship with the natural rhythms of life—birth, death, renewal. Menstruation was referred to in negative terms like "the curse" and women were treated as such. Moon cycles, and seasons replaced reverence with control. In doing so, it suppressed the Sacred Feminine and planted resistance into the body, psyche, and spirit. The result is an ongoing inner and societal war between domination and flow, structure and intuition, hierarchy and harmony.

The more we cling to one all-powerful masculine male god, instead of seeing god as the source of all life force energy, the more we drift from the wisdom of the womb, the soil, and the sacred dance of balance.

Faith is an inner compass. It is fluid, intuitive, and deeply personal. It is a tool of Sacred Feminine energy because it arises not from fear or force, but from trust, embodiment, and inner knowing. Sacred Feminine is faith and it flows with the rhythms of nature, honors the unknown and embraces connection to self, others, and the divine in all things. It is not bound by dogma, but guided by reverence. This kind of faith invites unity, nurtures wholeness, and births wisdom across generations.

In contrast, when monotheism became a tool of empire and control, it morphed into an expression of imbalanced masculine energy. Rigid, hierarchical, and externalized. Rather than inviting communion with the sacred, it imposed obedience to a singular male god, often positioned as a judge or ruler. This model is the blueprint that was devised to divide the sacred spirit from the body, the Earth, the feminine, and even from the conscious awareness. It replaced direct spiritual experience with intermediaries and institutions, and replaced divine mystery with law, punishment, and exclusion.

This imbalance has deeply traumatized both individuals and societies. At the individual level, it fractures identity especially in women who carry feminine energy in abundance by teaching them to mistrust their intuition, deny their connection to their own bodies, and seek worth through submission to outside sources.

At the societal level, it fuels division and conflict, religious and racial supremacy, and the violent policing of culture, race, gender, sexuality, and systems of belief in order to maintain absolute power and control.

The trauma this creates manifests as anxiety, shame, disconnection, generational imbalance and loss of humanity. Instead of healing, we perform in life like robots. Instead of belonging, we mindlessly obey. And instead of evolving, we resist the very energy that could restore us.

The demonization of feminine wisdom, intuition, and earth-based spirituality—seen in historical witch hunts and cultural erasure.

As the Sacred Feminine was suppressed, so too were the values of compassion, collaboration, and cyclical living. The world began to favor linear growth over sustainable rhythms—and humanity has been out of balance ever since.

The Call for Integration: Honoring Both Energies

We are now at a tipping point. A society led solely by masculine energy and stripped of the balancing force of the Sacred Feminine becomes rigid, exploitative, and disconnected.

But a society that honors both the Sacred Feminine and the Divine Masculine can heal and regenerate.

The Divine Masculine, in its sacred form, protects, provides, builds structure, and upholds truth. When it walks in partnership with the feminine, it becomes a force for justice rather than control.

We don't need to recreate the past, we need an inner evolution in order to evolve in ways that support spiritual, physical and emotional balance and lights the pathway to wisdom, compassion and love.

We need:

- Leaders who are emotionally intelligent and intuitively guided.
- Systems built not just for efficiency, but for wellness and inner beauty.
- Spirituality that includes connection to the body, the Earth, and the cycles of life.
- A return to soft power—the kind that transforms from within.

Chapter 10:

Enter Into Her Gates with Thanksgiving and Into Her Courts with Praise

There was a time when society was organized around rigid structures—limited choices, clear roles. While that offered predictability, it often came at the cost of authenticity, freedom, and deeper emotional connection.

Today, we live in a world overflowing with choices yet starved for meaning.

Roles have dissolved, institutions are crumbling, and people are being called to redefine identity without a map.

This in-between space is both a portal and a pressure point.

At the root of this collective disorientation lies a deeper issue: the chronic suppression of sacred balance—the harmony between feminine and masculine energy in individuals and in the systems we create. We've inherited a world built on imbalance. And the symptoms are everywhere.

Look at the rise in authoritarianism globally—leaders consolidating power, silencing opposition, and ruling through dominance, not compassion. This is wounded masculine energy: control without care, action without reflection. Sacred Masculine energy builds, protects, and leads with integrity, but when it is disconnected from the Sacred Feminine's intuition, empathy, and humility—it becomes force without conscience.

Similarly, observe the mental health crisis sweeping across generations. Depression, anxiety, burnout, emotional disconnection—all intensified by the glorification of hustling, hyper-productivity, and emotional ignorance. These are societies where the Sacred Feminine resources have been deemed weak or inconvenient. When we suppress the feminine, we lose our ability to feel, to grieve, to be present with our own humanity.

This suppression also manifests in intimate relationships. A generation raised without emotional literacy struggles to build healthy connections. We see it in the rise of toxic relationship dynamics, where people oscillate between emotional dependency and emotional avoidance. When men are taught that strength is domination, and women are taught to be pleasing instead of spiritually powerful, intimacy becomes a battlefield instead of a sanctuary.

The Personal is Political—and Energetic

The Sacred Feminine and Masculine are not about gender—they are energetic archetypes within us all. When they are suppressed, we create fractured identities: men afraid to be vulnerable, women afraid to take up space, people unsure of how to integrate emotion with intellect, softness with strength.

In politics, we see this fracture in leaders who seek absolute power with no accountability. Consider regimes that suppress women's rights while weaponizing hyper-masculine rhetoric. Or tech billionaires reshaping the world without spiritual or emotional intelligence—power without wisdom.

When power is not rooted in sacred balance, it becomes extractive, not regenerative. It takes without replenishing. That is why we see climate destruction, economic greed, and technological advancement without ethical grounding.

The Sacred Feminine as Medicine

Reclaiming Sacred Feminine energy does not mean rejecting masculine energy—it means restoring balance. The Sacred Feminine invites us to slow down, feel, listen, nurture, and remember our interconnectedness. It brings us back to the body, to breath, to ritual, to compassion.

Sacred Feminine energy helps us repair ourselves. It tells us:

- You do not need to perform to be loved.
- Rest is not laziness.
- Your emotions are messengers, not enemies.

When this energy is restored, the masculine is no longer reactive or violent. It becomes protective, disciplined, visionary, and strong in a way that includes tenderness. This is the warrior who listens, the leader who rests, the father who cries, the mother whose voice is honored and respected.

A Sacred Feminine Invocation of Return

We have long been taught to enter temples with bowed heads, knees bent in guilt, and hearts heavy with shame. But the Sacred Feminine temple does not ask you to shrink. She asks you to remember.

To come into her gates with thanksgiving is not merely wise and poetic—it is spiritual instruction.

It is the call to approach the Divine Feminine with gratitude instead of guilt, presence instead of performance. It is a reclamation of the ancient truth: that the body is a temple, the womb is a portal, and the feminine is holy—not in spite of her blood, tears, and rhythms, but because of them.

The Return to the Sacred Feminine Court

In the distorted masculine world, praise is often conditional and based on status, achievement, or external worth. But in the courts of the Sacred Feminine, praise is not earned. It is inherent.

You were born of her.

Born through her.

You are, even now, embraced by her.

To return to her courts with praise is to recognize the divine in the cycles of your life, the highs and the lows, the joy and pain, the wins and losses. It is to know that holiness lives not only in the high moments, but also in the moments that are humbling and cause feelings of defeat, sorrow and disappointment.

Praise does not wait for your perfection.

She celebrates your process.

She delights in your devotion.

She dances to your prayers, even when they're wordless.

Thanksgiving as Sacred Frequency

Gratitude is not just a polite feeling, it is an energetic gateway. When you give thanks, you align your vibration with abundance. You shift from lack to love, from fear to flow.

When you say, "Thank you":

- You open your heart to receive.
- You soften the tight grip of control.

- You become a vessel through which divine blessings can pour into.

The Sacred Feminine responds to gratitude like the ocean tides to the moon. She is cleansed and replenished through the process of becoming full and then releasing.

Give thanks for your body, not just when it looks a certain way, but for carrying you through as you are becoming.

Give thanks for your emotions, not just when they feel light, but for their wisdom, their guidance and their truth.

Give thanks for your intuition, those quiet whispers of your highest self that lead you back to your path when the world shouts distractions.

Praise as Sacred Power

In the Sacred Feminine realm, praise is not about flattery, it is a spiritual technology. It is how we rewire our inner world to remember the divine pattern beneath all things.

When you praise:

- You shift the narrative from victimhood to victory.
- You lift your voice in alignment with the frequency of miracles.
- You affirm what is sacred even in the midst of struggle.

Praise the source that created you.

Praise the womb that cultivated you.

Praise the Earth that sustains you.

Praise the Spirit within you that refuses to be silenced.

Praise is the Sacred Feminine form of power—it doesn't conquer, softens through vulnerability, magnetizes and attracts. It doesn't dominate, it radiates. It doesn't perform, it remembers.

Embodied Invitation

To live this chapter of your life is to move through your days as both priestess and temple. You are not waiting to be allowed in because your treasure is already inside. You are not asking to be chosen—you were chosen before time began.

Let this be your sacred practice:

- Wake with thanksgiving. Before the day begins, thank your body for waking. Thank your breath for returning.
- Enter your daily routines as rituals. Cooking, bathing, journaling. Make them sacred acts. Fill them with presence.
- Offer praise often. Speak blessings over your body. Over your work. Over your relationships. Praise rewrites your story and shifts your atmosphere.

Heaven's Feminine Gate

"Come into her gates with thanksgiving, and into her courts with praise" is not only scriptural; it is blueprint. A path to healing. A way home.

For through those gates, you remember that holiness is not distant.

It lives in your hips, your hands, your heart.

Through those courts, you remember that the Sacred Feminine is not a metaphor, but your birthright, your guide, your inner sanctuary.

Walk in with thanksgiving.

Stand strong and vulnerable in praise.

And know: the sacred was never far away.

She was always within you, waiting to be welcomed home.

The pendulum has historically swung between masculine and feminine dominance.

It's time for the pendulum to find balance and become still.

Fertility has always been at the core of human evolution. Goddess energy has prioritized, actualized and legitimized fertility. Sexual and sensual energy was the prevailing wisdom and focus of the ancient world. Source energy honors and desires goddess energy.

Biblical scripture draws the analogy of God being the bridegroom and the church or temple being the bride.

A goddess' body is most certainly a temple, a storehouse of treasure and a magical place where life is created and brought forth.

Creation is honored through procreation as well as through order and balance.

Women and men lost their ability to honor the creator and creation through outside influences.

The allegory of Adam and Eve depicts the serpent playing the role of the material world. It tempts the two to focus their attention and energy on the exogenous world.

The serpent gives Adam and Eve a glimpse of life beyond the borders of provision and entitlement.

Beyond their borders, there would be even more abundance, and more sensory and choices to experience.

He converted them from creatures of "being" energy, which is an internal, endogenous connection to all that is, into creatures that embrace the energy of striving and doing from a place of competition, greed and exogenous connection to the 3D material world.

Being energy acknowledges and honors creation, and the source of creation, while "doing" energy, without the inspiration that is derived from honoring creation to accompany it, lacks balance and grace.

It is in the imbalance of feminine "being" energy and masculine "doing" energy that human beings are dishonored, disgraced and lose their god/goddess nature leaving them feeling naked and afraid.

When feelings of self-love, abundance, pleasure, sensuality and sexuality are scarce or missing completely, you will feel energies of victimization and a sense of lack.

This imbalance, or perversion is reflected in relationships between a man and a woman, neighbors, parent and child, extended families, communities, and between nations.

When men remember to honor the goddess, feminine consciousness and understand "soft power," they will remember their original purpose and honor life.

When balance returns, you will begin experiencing pleasure in childbirth once again and redefine the power of your body as a temple and understand the true power of your blood as a place where codes, memories and mindsets are stored.

You determine your choices by establishing your mindset based on your memory of your identity.

Sacred Feminine, goddess energy will help you value life and control how, when and with whom you partner with in order to bring forth life.

Love is the supreme force, and when born of it, genetic coding is established, generational patterns are broken and new mindsets are formed that value, honor and protect life. Never allow anyone or anything to enter your gates without it!

The Power of Oneness (We are One)

Holy books are filled with codes that help us to access our identity and purpose. There is nothing new under the sun.

Everything on and within the earth reflects the heavens, other universes and solar systems. Mimicry or patterns of duplication are all around us. As above, so below and as within so without.

The carrot mimics the iris of the human eye, the tomato mimics the chambers of the human heart, the automobile engine is patterned after the human cardiovascular system, the airplane was designed by mimicking the aeronautics of birds.

The laws of the universe govern the human body. Your thoughts impact your brain and the brain conducts the execution of the body.

There is cooperation and balance in the heavens as well as within the universe called the human body.

The relationship between masculine and feminine holds immense power. Masculine need females in order to gain greater access to the Divine Feminine, become whole and truly purposeful. Feminine need to be praised, honored and adored by her male counterpart in order to give access to immense treasures of creative forces residing within her courts. The Divine Feminine is complex. It is not as effective when dominated. It can become oppressed and suppressed giving way to ego for survival.

Every schism in the mind, disease in the body and division in society manifests from the external stressors of a toxic, masculine and patriarchal core belief that life is about competition and survival of the fittest rather than the divine truth that the earth is abundant and thriving.

Depletion is based in the ignorance of sacred cycles and the greed caused by the flawed belief lack is naturally occurring rather than it being a byproduct of greed.

Fear creates stress and stress creates psychological and social imbalance causing many to dishonor mother earth and her inhabitants interrupting their ability to thrive.

Thriving can only take place through the compassion, love and nurturing of divine Sacred Feminine energy and goddess consciousness.

Love is the principal thing and it helps human beings reconstitute and remember their true nature.

Returning to Your Divine Identity

Whomever defines your identity possesses your power!

Before I delve further into how you might gain or regain your power, let's discuss your identity. Everything you know as a human being has been bequeathed to you from ancestors, customs and cultures, myths and legends. Subliminal messages about your identity are constantly communicated through systems of politics, religion and education. Most people have never cultivated a single conscious thought born out of a deep desire for an answer to a burning question. Many people simply identify themselves from within the boundaries of what is, rather than what might be in the realm of possibility.

The purpose of our being is to expand and evolve. The human species has been evolving physically, chemically, emotionally, mentally and spiritually from the moment of our existence. It's how we're able to not only survive, but also thrive. Our desire to solve problems, create what we desire and meet our needs ignite a cascade of corresponding energy. It is the flame and flicker of energy that blaze pathways of new thought, new understanding and new states of being. You were born to think, ask, desire and manifest from a place of wholeness and inspiration. You cannot become whole in the knowledge of your identity without becoming autonomous. You cannot become autonomous without fully embracing self-love. Self-love is knowing and understanding that you are the answer. You embody the solution. It is in knowing from within the fibers of your being that you have been appointed to a time and space of abundance.

Abundance is in you, with you and all about you. You are the embodiment of abundance, and that truth will fill you with self-confidence, gratitude and love.

The question that I posed to my loving mother as a child had nothing to do with anything that existed outside of me. There was a divine spark burning deep within my happy little heart that had been ignited before I was born, and I wanted to fully embrace it as my own. I was sure that it was a source of a beautiful, joyous and wondrous life. I know that my mother didn't want me to become a target for those willing to put me in my place with words like, "Who do you think you are?" or "You think you're something" or "You're too big for your britches." Words that I would often hear in my lifetime from strangers as well as those that claim to love me, but instead chose to curse me. Words that in truth are not simply words, but spells and the true meaning of cursing.

There were always systemic programs beckoning me away from my uniqueness and pushing me toward conformity. I know that the reason I always felt unique and divinely purposed is because I can feel the connection to my divine design, my sacred codes called DNA. My DNA houses a library of experiences of those that came before me as well as my own personal experiences from a time that I can no longer consciously remember.

There are codes built into institutions and systems of education every day. They encourage staying within the group and within the standard guidelines and status quo, coloring within the lines and waiting until you are recognized before you speak, as well as accepting someone else's idea of what is vital information. None of the aforementioned are conducive to cultivating a sacred being, but instead deliberately undermines your autonomy and sovereignty.

Sacred Practices for Inner Healing

Ayurveda's holistic approach to health and wellness includes personalized nutritional plans, herbal remedies, and lifestyle modifications. It offers significant benefits for both physical and emotional well-being.

By addressing the root causes of imbalances and promoting harmony in the body and mind, Ayurveda can help individuals achieve long-term health and resilience by restoring wholeness and consciousness, your ground state.

The Societal Impact of Emotional Instability

Emotional instability, often manifesting as mental health issues such as anxiety, depression, and mood disorders, has significant societal impacts. In 2021, about 22.8% of U.S. adults experienced any mental illness (AMI), with a higher prevalence in young adults. This widespread prevalence leads to numerous societal challenges.

Firstly, emotional instability affects productivity and economic stability. Individuals with mental health issues often face difficulties in maintaining employment, leading to reduced workforce participation and increased absenteeism. This can result in significant economic costs due to lost productivity and increased healthcare expenses. For instance, untreated mental health conditions can lead to chronic stress, affecting physical health and increasing the burden on healthcare systems.

Secondly, emotional instability significantly impacts family dynamics and child development. Children exposed to unstable environments due to parental mental health issues are at greater risk of developing behavioral and emotional problems themselves. The CDC highlights that adverse childhood experiences (ACEs), such as living with a mentally ill parent, can lead to long-term health and social issues.

Furthermore, the COVID-19 pandemic and our current political climate have exacerbated emotional instability, with increased reports of anxiety, depression, and prolonged grief disorder due to isolation and loss. The mental health system is currently overwhelmed, struggling to meet the rising demand for services. While telehealth has expanded access, the system remains under strain.

Overall, emotional instability affects not just the individuals experiencing it but also has broader societal implications, including economic costs, family and community health, and increased demand on healthcare services. Addressing these challenges requires comprehensive mental health strategies, including early intervention, improved access to care, and supportive community resources beyond the modern healthcare systems.

Understanding Ourselves as Sentient and Sensory Beings

To truly awaken to the power of Sacred Feminine energy, we must begin by honoring our nature as sentient and sensory beings—fully alive, emotionally intelligent, and spiritually connected. Through this awareness, we can recognize how the five elements (earth, water, fire, air, and ether) flow through our bodies and lives, mirroring the rhythms of nature and our own inner cycles.

Each of our senses—sight, sound, touch, taste, and smell—serves as a sacred portal. They ground us in the present moment and connect us with the divine essence of life. When we listen to our bodies, emotions, and intuitive knowing, we begin to decode the wisdom encoded in our experiences.

As we deepen our relationship with the elements and our senses, we reclaim our ability to:

- Transform ourselves through conscious embodiment and emotional healing.
- Raise children with emotional balance, autonomy and spiritual integrity.
- Attract healthy partners and relationships rooted in authenticity and respect.
- Heal families and communities by modeling wholeness, compassion, and sacred balance.

This is the work of the Sacred Feminine—to alchemize, nurture, and uplift not only ourselves, but everyone we touch. When we reclaim our softness as power, our intuition as guidance, and our emotions as sacred messengers, we become catalysts for generational transformation.

Conclusion:

A Society Reborn

Heaven on Earth: The Sacred Task of Embodiment

"On Earth as it is in Heaven."

This is not just a prayer.

It is a divine assignment.

We are not here to escape Earth for Heaven.

We are here to anchor Heaven into Earth.

Heaven is not elsewhere.

Heaven is not a place we go after death. Heaven is a frequency—a state of divine harmony, love, justice, and sacred order. It is the reality of wholeness before trauma, before power distorted love, before fear overshadowed the soul.

Heaven is a memory encoded in the spirit.

It is a truth we carry deep in our bones.

And Earth—this physical plane—is the sacred ground where that truth longs to take form.

But we have forgotten.

In forgetting, we have built systems that serve separation over unity.

We have created cultures that reward competition over compassion.

We have learned to suppress the Sacred Feminine—the presence that reminds us to slow down, feel deeply, and live in alignment with soul, not ego.

And yet, something ancient is returning.

A remembering. A rebalancing. A resurrection.

The Feminine Brings Heaven Closer

It is the Sacred Feminine energy that first begins the descent of Heaven into Earth. She is the bridge between the invisible and the visible, the inner world and the outer expression.

She whispers:

- "You are not separate from the Divine."
- "Your body is holy."
- "Your rest, your tears, your intuition are gateways, not distractions."

Through her, we remember that love is not weakness—it is law. That stillness is not laziness—it is power. That healing is not indulgence—it is service to all life.

When we honor the Sacred Feminine, we restore the soul of the world.

And when we unite her with the Sacred Masculine, we birth sacred action.

This is when Heaven begins to descend.

Heaven Comes Through the Body

Heaven does not arrive through abstract belief or distant prophecy.

Heaven arrives through your nervous system, your breath, your choices.

It arrives:

- When you pause instead of react.
- When you forgive instead of punish.
- When you create beauty instead of feeding chaos.
- When you parent, lead, and love from presence, not performance.

The body becomes the temple.

The heart becomes the altar.

The breath becomes the prayer.

You are not just waiting for Heaven. You are becoming it.

The End of Hierarchy, The Rise of Harmony

To bring Heaven to Earth is to dissolve the old paradigm of hierarchy and domination—the distorted masculine that separates the sacred from the everyday, the divine from the human, spirit from flesh.

In the old model, power was vertical—someone above, someone below.

In the new sacred model, power is circular—shared, honored, and embodied.

We no longer look to temples built by men to find God.

We look to the body, the Earth, the mother, the moment.

This is what Sacred Feminine leadership does.

It reminds us that Heaven is not a city, it's a state of consciousness that reflects a divine rhythm. It is a visible manifestation of balance.

It is justice with a heart. It is the truth in our tears and the power of your presence.

A Sacred Society Begins within You

To rebuild society is to transform the soul.

You bring Heaven to Earth when:

- You speak truth in kindness.
- You build businesses that honor life.
- You raise children who trust their intuition.
- You honor your pleasure as holy.
- You turn your healing into a medicine for others.

This is soft power.

This is sacred leadership and guidance.

This is Heaven in motion.

Heaven is not a myth. It is the world we build when we choose love over fear, balance over domination, embodiment over avoidance.

And it begins right here, in your breath, in your body, in the sacred now.

The Role of Women in Restoring Balance

There is a sacred truth the world has tried to forget: that women are the original stewards of balance, harmony, and divine order.

For far too long, feminine energy has been silenced, shamed, or forced to take a masculine form in order to survive. Women have been conditioned to prove their worth through productivity, perfection, and performance, while their intuitive, emotional, and cyclical nature was deemed too soft, too irrational, or too inconvenient for modern life. But deep within every woman lies a reservoir of ancient wisdom and a wellspring of sacred power that, once reawakened, has the capacity to restore balance to a broken world.

The rise of Sacred Feminine energy is not a trend. It is a return, a remembering. Women, when yielded to and aligned with sacred energy in its masculine and feminine forms, expressions, and stages, are the key component in supporting a healthy society.

When a woman reconnects with her sacred energy, she doesn't just heal herself. She sends out a vibration that touches everything around her. Her presence softens the hardened. Her intuition reveals hidden truths. Her nurturing energy invites others into wholeness. She births not only life, but ideas, healing, and transformation.

This is the real power of the feminine: it does not seek to dominate, it seeks to harmonize. It does not need a throne, because it is the throne. It does not overpower, it overflows. And in this overflowing, it creates space for all to evolve, heal and emerge as a new creation.

The feminine way of leading is not rooted in hierarchy, but in sacred reciprocity. It sees community as essential, not optional. It listens deeply. It moves in rhythm with nature. It honors the unseen. It leaves space for rest, for ritual, for the soul to catch up with the body.

Reclaiming this power takes courage. In a world that rewards the performance of masculine energy, it is radical to slow down. To feel. To say no. To nurture. To create from the womb instead of the mind. Many women carry generational trauma that tells them their softness is weakness. Many have been told that their emotions are a liability, that their desires are too much, or that their magic is dangerous.

And yet, the world is starving for what women carry.

The Sacred Feminine energy within women is what brings the masculine back into the right relationship. It teaches protection without control, provision without exploitation, power without oppression. Women are not here to fight the old systems, they are here to outgrow them, to replace them with something rooted in wisdom, ritual, and divine alignment.

To restore balance in the world, women must first restore balance within themselves. This means healing their relationship with their own femininity—learning to trust their intuition, honor their emotions, reconnect with their bodies, and reclaim their sacred cycles. It means supporting other women in their transformation, without competition or comparison. It means mothering not just children, but visions, communities, and sacred futures.

This emergence is not exclusive to women by gender, it is a sacred invitation extended to everyone, because we all have access to feminine energy. But women, especially those who have been silenced, marginalized, or underestimated, hold a critical role in awakening this divine frequency.

Let us remember: when women heal, families heal. When women transform, communities will transform. When women awaken, the Earth feels protected and provided for and she responds in kind.

This is your invitation.

You are not too late. You are right on time. The Sacred Feminine is not something you must acquire; it is already within you, waiting to be remembered.

And when women remember who they are, the world remembers what it was created to become.

Imagine a world where policy is shaped by compassion as much as data. Where collaboration outshines competition. Where feminine and masculine energies are not weaponized, but harmonized. Where power is not domination, but responsibility and accountability.

That is what Sacred Feminine energy is calling us to birth.

It begins with you, the temple of the divine spark, the daughter of creation and the sacred transformative weapon of soft power!

Closing Affirmations, Prayers & Meditation

Repeat aloud or write in your journal each day to anchor sacred truth into your being:

- I am the embodiment of Sacred Feminine wisdom.
- I am soft power and radiant strength.
- I trust my inner knowing and honor the rhythm of my soul.
- I choose nurturing over performance, presence over perfection.
- I create balance within, and it ripples into the world.
- My softness is not weakness—it is a divine force.
- I am a vessel of healing for my lineage and my community.
- I rise with grace. I lead with love. I am becoming sacred.

Closing Prayer for Sacred Feminine Emergence

Divine Mother, Ancient One, Holy Presence,

We thank you for awakening what has long been buried.

We thank you for the remembrance of truth, of power, of softness, of rhythm.

Wrap us in your infinite grace as we walk boldly toward balance.

May our hearts remain open, our bodies grounded, and our spirits aligned.

May we raise daughters who know their worth and sons who honor the sacred.

May our lives be altars where healing continues,

where presence overflows,

where love never hides.

Let this sacred work extend beyond the page—

into homes, circles, institutions, and lands.

Let it be alive in how we mother, how we speak, how we serve.

May we never forget: we are the womb of the new world.

And so it is.

Guided Meditation: A Society Reborn Through Me

Begin in stillness. Place one hand on your heart, the other on your womb (or solar plexus). Close your eyes.

Breathe deeply in through the nose, out through the mouth. Feel your body soften with every breath.

Now, in your mind's eye, envision a world that is whole.

A world where every child is loved without condition.

Where the feminine is honored. Where the masculine is healed.

Where balance isn't forced, but flows.

See yourself as a vessel of that world.

Not separate from it but central to it.

Whisper silently or aloud:

I am a guardian of sacred balance.

The love I hold becomes the world I live in.

I am rebirthing a new Earth through the frequency I carry.

I am sacred. I am soft power. I am the new way.

Inhale and Exhale

Feel it settle in your bones.

When you are ready, open your eyes and return—changed.

Author's Bio

Lorrie Ann Fluker is a transformative voice in sacred feminine healing and personal alchemy. With over 20 years of experience in strategy, community development and advocacy, Lorrie blends her expertise in Ayurvedic health education, sacred feminine balance, and ancestral practices to guide women—especially women of color—toward reclaiming their inner strength and aligning with their divine purpose.

She is the founder of *I Am Soft Power, LLC*, a wellness brand focused on sacred feminine energy and holistic living. Lorrie's offerings, including her book *Becoming Sacred*, empower and enlighten women to not only cultivate sacred feminine energy that directly affects personal health and wellness, but to also support the emergence of sacred balance, health and wellness within their family and community, thereby creating a ripple effect of conscious awareness, sacred balance and renewal on the earth.

Lorrie's life is a testament to resilience, reverence, and reinvention, with a deep commitment to healing, transformation, and community.